European History Stories

*50 True and Fascinating Tales of Major
Events and People from Europe's Past*

Table of Contents

INTRODUCTION...1
CHAPTER 1: STORIES FROM ANCIENT GREECE...3
CHAPTER 2: STORIES OF THE ROMAN EMPIRE 14
CHAPTER 3: STORIES OF HOW CHRISTIANITY SPREAD 25
CHAPTER 4: VIKING EXPEDITIONS AND THEIR STORIES 35
CHAPTER 5: STORIES OF A BLACK DEATH MOST DEADLY...................44
CHAPTER 6: RENAISSANCE STORIES...53
CHAPTER 7: EXPLORATION AND EXPANSION STORIES 63
CHAPTER 8: ENLIGHTENMENT, RETRIBUTION, AND
REVOLUTION STORIES...73
CHAPTER 9: NAPOLEON BONAPARTE: STORIES OF HIS RISE AND
FALL...83
CHAPTER 10: STORIES OF ADOLF HITLER..93
CONCLUSION..102
CHECK OUT ANOTHER BOOK IN THE SERIES....................................104
REFERENCES 105

Introduction

You will embark on a journey through the chronicles of history as you read this book. You'll find captivating stories full of triumphs, challenges, and tribulations. This book explores key historical moments that have shaped the modern world using comprehensive, enlightening narratives that bridge the past, present, and future. What sets this book apart is that it offers an extensive view of European history, spanning different periods.

From the birth of democracy in Athen's Agora to the Holocaust, this book delves into transformative, enlightening, inspiring, and devastating historical moments. You will traverse the rise and fall of empires in Europe, the emergence and spread of religions, the outburst of revolutions, and the exploits of rulers and explorers. The stories of prominent individuals and historical events, along with the profound effects and consequences of their doings, will unfold in each chapter.

Your journey will take off in the birthplace of democracy: Ancient Greece. You'll learn about the structure of the nation's city-states and gain insight into the societal reforms that gave rise to democracy. The book illustrates the pros and cons of this political system and explains the roles of the citizenry, along with other political components, in the enduring legacy of Athenian democracy.

The book will then guide you through Julius Caesar's early life, his ascent to power, and notable achievements, leading you all the way to his assassination and enduring influence on the Roman Empire and beyond. You'll then learn how Christianity spread in Europe, trace the early

Christian communities, and dive into the world of missionary journeys and the challenges that arose along the way.

You'll dig into the realm of Norsemen and Vikings, their motivations and remarkable journeys, and the far-reaching influence they left in Europe. Your expedition will take a harrowing turn as you learn about the Black Death, its origins, how it spread, and its life-altering consequences.

Fortunately, the book will pick up a more upbeat tone as it steers you toward the Renaissance and the influence of prominent families on the culture, politics, and economics of the time. You'll jump into the Age of Exploration and uncover the narratives of explorers like Columbus, da Gama, and Magellan as they navigated new horizons, leading to the rise of colonial empires.

You'll embrace the Age of Enlightenment and learn about the interesting philosophical ideas of Voltaire, Rousseau, and Kant and their influence on notable revolutions. You'll then discover Napoleon Bonaparte's extraordinary journey from obscurity to absolute power and explore his military successes and the lasting impact his efforts had on Europe. Finally, you'll encounter the distressing legacy of Hitler, reading into his rise and rule and the calamities he inflicted.

Chapter 1: Stories from Ancient Greece

This chapter explores the rich tapestry of ancient Greece's social, political, and philosophical life that led to the birth of democracy. It delves into the structure of the city-state, uncovering its landmarks and unique governance and focusing on Athens as the beacon of early democratic practice. Reading this chapter, you'll understand how democracy emerged and learn about the societal reforms that made it possible.

You'll learn about the benefits and drawbacks of the Athenian democracy and how it affected individuals and society at large. You'll learn about the roles of the citizenry, the Assembly, the Council of Five Hundred, and how their decisions guided Athenian life. Finally, the chapter uncovers how the legacy of Athenian democracy is significant to modern democratic principles.

1. The Structure of the City-State

Ancient Greece comprised numerous city-states, known as polis, which set down the community structure. Each polis had an urban center, protected by walls and surrounded by rural grounds. While all of them were in the same nation, each city-state had its own governing laws. All urban centers were home to government buildings and temples, usually built on a hill known as an acropolis. The Athenian Parthenon, built in honor of Athena, the goddess of wisdom, is an example of an acropolis.

The cities were rich in culture and political activities and served as the center of commerce and trade, which is why they were home to the majority of the population.

Ancient Greece was made up of numerous city-states.
Γ. Ψάλτης, Public domain, via Wikimedia Commons.
https://commons.wikimedia.org/wiki/File:Map_of_Athens,_1890.jpg

Although there were over 1000 ancient Greek city-states, Athens, Sparta, Thebes, Aegina, Corinth, Syracuse, Eretria, Rhodes, Argos, and Elis were the 10 main ones. Each polis' ruling style, philosophies, and way of life were unique. For instance, while Athenians were known for their love of art and knowledge, Sparta was characterized by its strong military and government. Greece's geography and physical features were likely among the reasons why this community and political structure were developed. The mountains and rocky terrain caused people to form separate and independent communities. The sea was a relatively easier medium of communication than land. Additionally, the aristocrats believed it was easier to spot and eliminate tyrants if they maintained independent city-states rather than a central monarchy.

2. Cleisthenes: The Father of Athenian Democracy

The word *democracy* is derived from the term *demokratia,* which refers to a political system influenced by the general public. The first half of the term comes from the word demos, which translates to the people. The other half is derived from kratos, which means power. Cleisthenes developed This political reform system in 507 BC, becoming the world's first-ever democracy.

Cleisthenes, the father of Athenian democracy.
http://www.ohiochannel.org/, Attribution, via Wikimedia Commons:
https://commons.wikimedia.org/wiki/File:Cleisthenes.jpg

Demokratia had three components: the ekklesia, the boule, and the dikasteria. The Ekklesia was a sovereign body in the government that wrote laws and foreign policies. They also had the power to practice ostracism, which refers to the act of expelling someone from Athens for a decade. The boule was a council that consisted of representatives from the ten tribes of Athens. The *dikasteria* referred to the courts where citizens took their arguments and presented their cases before jurors. This political invention still shapes the lives of millions of people worldwide millennia later.

One of the greatest achievements that Cleisthenes, the father of democracy, amounted to was that the Athenian aristocrats no longer had autonomous power over political decisions. He also eliminated the distinction between them and the low- and middle-working class who were in the army and navy.

According to Herodotus, Cleisthenes' innovation has made all people equal before the law. In reality, however, this equality didn't apply to the entire ancient Athenian population because only men older than 18 were allowed to participate in democratic procedures. There were around 250,000 citizens in Athena in the 4th century, only 40,000 of whom were men over 18.

3. The Agora: The Heart of Athenian Life and Politics

The Agora lies in the bustling center of ancient Athens. This marketplace captured the essence of ancient Greek life and politics. The Agora, considered the heart of the city-state, was where trade and commerce procedures occurred, and culture and democracy emerged.

The Agora, a busy, open space located at the base of the Acropolis, was the physical hub that gathered the Athenian population. It accommodated a wide range of activities, including many political gatherings, social interactions, and religious rituals. Merchants arrived at the Agora from all over the Mediterranean to trade all kinds of goods, from textiles and pottery to precious metals and spices. This marketplace was crucial to Athens' economic life and was among the most important streams of Greek capital. While most ancient Greek city-states had an Agora, none were as famous or large as the one found in Athens.

The Athenian Agora both directly and indirectly influenced modern-day trade and commerce procedures. Today's online or brick-and-mortar marketplaces still reflect the basic principles of exchange and trade that merchants conducted in the Agora. This ancient marketplace also offers valuable insights and information regarding the development and evolution of early economies, trade practices, and civic life. This might influence how today's economic and political issues are addressed, allowing responsible entities to make informed decisions.

The Agora was not only a marketplace and political hub but also a cultural and intellectual center. There, you can find the Stoa of Attalos, rebuilt in the 20th century. This colonnade used to house numerous schools of philosophy and was where philosophical debates and discussions occurred. The Agora was adorned with sculptures, pottery, and other incredible works of art. Artisans also displayed and traded their masterpieces there. Poets and scholars gathered alongside artists, creating an environment of cultural exchange, beauty, and creativity in the marketplace.

The Agora was also associated with religious life and practices, as it was home to various temples and altars dedicated to numerous deities. The Hephaisteion, a temple that honors the deity Hephaestus, still stands today. Religious rituals, celebrations, sacrifices, and festivals were essential aspects of Athenian traditions and identity – and usually took place in the Agora.

On top of all these functions, the Agora was a place where people could meet and make friends every day. The marketplace offered several food and beverage options, and civilians went there to hang out, engage in discussions, and share news. The Agora is a melting pot, proving that art, social interactions, politics, religion, and commerce can co-exist and thrive together.

4. The Pnyx: Where Democracy Took Center Stage

Jury members often met in the Agora to discuss eminent issues, share their opinions and concerns, and simply bond. This social hub featured a large assembly area, the Pnyx, making the Agora a center of life and politics. Athenian members of the Assembly gathered at the Pnyx to discuss and vote on social and legal issues. The Athenian Agora is particularly historically significant because it was the birthplace of democracy.

The Pros and Cons of Ancient Athenian Democracy

The Pros of the New Political System

• It Increased Political Participation

Ancient Athenian democracy enabled citizens to actively participate in the political process. The portion of citizens who were allowed to partake in these procedures were able to share their opinions, vote and participate in the decision-making process, and propose legislation. Even if the entire population was not involved, the public still felt engaged and had a say in the policies and laws that shaped their lives. This fostered a sense of responsibility and control over their well-being and that of the state.

• It Was More Inclusive

Even if the new democratic system didn't apply to a large portion of the population, Cleisthenes' reforms still encouraged inclusivity because they extended beyond the traditional aristocracy. People who weren't of noble birth could now partake in these decisions, reducing the concentration of power among the nobles. This led to better social cohesion and contributed to the success of the polis.

• It Offered a Degree of Legal Protection

The new democratic system offered legal protection for citizens since it allowed them to seek redress for injustices and disagreements through fair and open trials. Everyone who believed they had been victims of violations was offered a degree of legal resources, enhancing the overall justice system and morale of the society.

The Cons of the New Political System

• It Offered Limited Public Participation

While the political system became more inclusive and encouraged political participation in comparison to earlier exclusively aristocratic systems, it was still very limited. The reforms only included men who fit certain criteria, such as having an Athenian bloodline or serving in the military. Women, slaves, and non-Athenians were excluded from the political system. Even though Cleisthenes' innovation gave more voice to the public, most members of the society couldn't share their opinions or defend and look out for their needs. This may have created further inequalities and marginalized groups within Athenian society.

• It Had the Potential for Demagoguery

Since citizens voted directly on important issues, there was always the possibility of demagogues manipulating public opinion for their own personal gain. They might have also pushed policies that prioritized their personal benefit and weren't in the city-state's long-term interest. The Athenian democracy was direct, making it more vulnerable to demagoguery, which raised concerns regarding the wisdom and stability of this political system.

• It Required a Significant Amount of Time and Resources

Partaking in the democratic political system required significant time and resources. Citizens who wished to vote and participate in the decision-making process had to serve on juries and attend assemblies, putting a strain on their work and family obligations. Those who tried to find a balance between personal and political commitments had limited participation in the democratic process, and those who couldn't dedicate adequate time and resources were excluded.

The Roles of the Citizenry, the Assembly, and the Council of Five Hundred

The citizenry, the Assembly, and the Council of Five Hundred played key roles in the ancient Athenian democratic system. Their contributions to the decision-making process guided all aspects of Athenian life, from daily administration matters to life-changing laws and policies.

The Citizenry

Only males over 18, free, and born to Athenian parents were granted Athenian citizenship after they served in the military for two years. Those who came from other city-states were treated as foreigners, and all women and slaves were excluded from citizenship. Citizens were granted rights and responsibilities in the democratic system and could vote on legislation, participate in the Assembly, and hold public office.

However, to attain and maintain these rights, they were expected to fulfill certain civic duties, such as dedicating the required time and resources to attending the Assembly when needed and serving in the military. The first form of democracy was characterized by its direct nature, where citizens were directly involved in decision-making. They were able to raise important matters and propose, vote, and debate laws and policies that affected the city-state and other members of the society.

5. The Assembly of Athens: The Voice of the People

The Assembly, also known as the Ekklesia, was the main Athenian democratic institution. It served as an open forum where all eligible citizens could meet, discuss, debate, and vote on important matters. However, convicts of self-prostitution, those who owed debt to the treasury, and those who failed to support or beat their family members were denied membership in the Assembly. All decisions made in the Assembly influenced aspects of Athenian life.

The Assembly gathered around 40 times per year at the Pnyx, an open-air auditorium, to address topics that spanned various areas in life, such as foreign policy, laws, financial matters, and the activities of public officials. All citizens could speak and participate in the Assembly, voice their concerns and opinions, and propose legislation, with those over 50 participating first. Major decisions were taken through majority votes, with the votes of all participants being presented and counted.

The Council of Five Hundred

The Council of Five Hundred, or the Boule, was an executive and administrative body that organized and implemented the Assembly's decisions and managed day-to-day affairs. Posting the locations and agendas of upcoming Assembly meetings was among their responsibilities.

The Boule was made up of 500 citizens, which consisted of 50 eligible individuals from the ten territorial units of Athens. Choosing the members was a relatively randomized process to lower the possibility of corruption. Members of this council only served one-year terms and couldn't serve more than twice in their lifetimes. This policy prevented the concentration of power among a few individuals. The Boule had several subcommittees that governed several areas, such as financial affairs, religious matters, and foreign affairs, ensuring the effective administration of the city-state.

How Their Decisions Guided Athenian Life

- Members of the Assembly proposed legislation, passed laws, and addressed policies that influenced daily life in Athens. They made decisions regarding foreign alliances and affairs, social regulations, trade, and taxation. The citizenry's direct involvement shaped the political and social landscapes at the time.

- The Boule ensured that all the decisions made by the Assembly were implemented. Members of this council managed public finances, oversaw the enforcement of laws, and organized military expeditions. They were cornerstones of the effectiveness of this political system.

- The Assembly and the Boule were held accountable to the citizenry. Citizens could practice ostracism or take legal actions against members of the Assembly or the Boule if they had taken unsatisfactory decisions or actions.

The Legacy of Athenian Democracy and Modern Democratic Principles

The Athenian democracy, which shaped the lives of ancient Greek civilians around 2,300 years ago, has served as a significant and everlasting stepping stone of the modern-day political and legal system. The Athenian democratic system has shaped today's democratic principles and practices that are enacted all across the globe. The following are a few ways in which the ancient Athenian democracy is eminent in contemporary democratic political structures:

The Participation and Influence of Citizens

Ancient Athenian democracy was characterized by direct citizen participation in political decision-making, while modern-day systems are more organized and are characterized by the use of representatives. Representatives ensure that citizens actively voice their concerns and participate in democratic processes while lowering the risk of demagoguery and reducing the time and resources that engaging in the political system requires.

While Athenian democracy set criteria for people allowed to participate in the democratic process, the use of representatives nowadays ensures that everyone of legal age can partake in the process.

The concept of popular sovereignty, which grants citizens ultimate political authority, also embodies the attributes of Athenian democracy.

Inclusive Political Systems

The shift from allowing only a narrow pool of aristocrats to participate in political decisions to giving power to a larger population segment was huge at the time. This reform laid the foundation for more inclusive political systems that foster civic equality. The fact that many people worldwide can now vote and participate in the legal decision-making process, regardless of their social status or birthplace, is the essence of democracy and was made possible by Cleisthenes' reform. This idea has led to the removal or diminishing of voting barriers, increased civil rights, and the fight against discrimination.

Laws That Reflect the Will of Citizens

Athenian democracy recognized the rule of law, a fundamental principle in democratic legal systems that stresses the importance of accountability, equality, transparency, and the protection of civilian rights. The rule of law holds all individuals accountable and equal before the law and provides fair and just legal processes. This rule also limits the power that the government has, making it crucial for maintaining justice and order and protecting the rights of the people and democratic principles.

Ancient Athenian laws were set forward by the Assembly and applied to all citizens impartially. Contemporary democratic processes continue to reflect the will of citizens and uphold equality and fairness. The ancient Athenian practice of holding government officials accountable through practices like ostracism and other legal actions contributed to the modern-day concept of government accountability and the checks and balances system.

Free Speech and Debate

The Assembly served as a public forum where eligible members could debate their opinions regarding laws and legislation and discuss various matters. Participants freely voted and deliberated on issues of importance. Modern democratic systems also encourage open discourse and free speech. It's believed that the exchange of ideas is vital for social and national welfare.

Grounds for Experimentation

The Athenian democratic model served as grounds for experimenting with democratic governance. Ancient Greek philosophers like Aristotle and Plato also inspired, critiqued, and analyzed Athenian democracy and offered invaluable insights into the strengths and weaknesses of the system. This allowed today's responsible parties to learn from past lessons and experiences and fine-tune them to suit modern life.

Ancient Athenian democracy resulted in lasting influence over global political systems, making them more inclusive and fostering greater political participation and legal protection. The democratic system at the time, however, also had drawbacks that modern entities could learn from. Athenian democracy limited those who could participate in political procedures by setting certain eligibility criteria, demanded significant time and resources, and was susceptible to demagoguery. Ancient Athenian democracy laid the foundation for refined democratic systems that transformed world politics.

Chapter 2: Stories of the Roman Empire

The Roman Empire has commanded the interest and attention of many historians and storytellers for centuries. It is hard to delve into the history of the eternal city without finding yourself caught up in a labyrinth of wonder and awe. Tales of legends, myths, and heroes woven together in the history of the birthplace of the Olympians.

Throughout history, poets, painters, and entertainers have adopted Rome as their muse to express their artistry. It is a fascinating story that never gets old, from its celebrated victories to its tales of woes.

You may ask yourself how this city of hills came to be the world's capital. There is a lot of controversy as to how this city came to life, not to mention the fact that many seem to have a different opinion on when it came to be

Romulus and Remus.

The Foundation of Roma

You may enjoy this tale if you're into mythology and majestic stories! Long ago, around 753 BC, Rome was founded by twin brothers Romulus and Remus.

The brothers were no ordinary humans; they were born of human mothers and fathered by the God of war, Mars. Shortly after their birth, King Amulius ordered their death by being placed in a basket and set free in the Tiber River to die of exposure and starvation.

The God of the River, Tiberinus, calmed the river tide to ensure the children's safety. As fate would have it, their basket would wash up on the river bank, where a female wolf stumbled upon them. The predator, against its own nature, nursed the young cubs until they were found by a shepherd. The shepherd took the children home to his wife, who decided to raise them as their own. Years passed, and the brothers became fit young men helping their adoptive father tend to the sheep. One day, they were confronted by the shepherds of the King, and a fight ensued.

As the stars would have it, they had a hand in defeating and killing the King who had tried to condemn them to death as infants. Time passed, and the twins decided to build a city together at the same spot where their basket had washed up on the Tiber River. Romulus wished to have Rome at the top of the Palatine Hill, while Remus favored the Aventine Hill. After failing to settle the disagreement peacefully, Romulus murdered his brother and fulfilled his wish of laying Rome's foundation on the Palatine Hill, becoming the first Roman King.

Now, if those tales have captured your interest, you should probably brace yourself for the saga of Julius Caesar.

6. From Rubicon to Rome: The Path of Caesar's Power

Before Rome was known as an Empire, it was a Republic and, before that, a land of kings. If we were to believe the olden tales, Rome was ruled by seven kings, starting with Romulus and ending with Lucius Tarquinius Superbus. The King was a symbol of leadership and religion. At his side, 300 Senators acted as advisors, helping and guiding the King's rule, but they had no real power.

The last King of Rome was proud and cruel, and hostile methods brought upon the end of the Etruscan power. The Senate and people rose against him and expelled him from the city, thus paving the way for the republic of Rome to come about.

The republic had a slightly different government. The people elected two consuls to serve for only one year; under the consuls were the 300 senators advising them. After completing their year of service, they were forbidden from filling the position again for 10 years. During the republic, the people were divided into classes, with the upper-class ruling. There were Patricians, Plebeians, and slaves.

Patricians were the wealthy; they usually lived in luxurious homes and had slaves serving their every need. They were free citizens allowed to attend the assembly and vote. The plebeians were also citizens of Rome but of a lower class, usually traders and craftsmen. They were also allowed to vote and attend assembly.

Slaves had no rights or wealth and weren't considered citizens. Like women at the time, they weren't allowed to go to assembly or vote. During times of crises like wars, it was a custom to name a dictator until the dust settled.

The Republic of Rome marked a time of prosperity and expansion until the arrival of Caesar.

Gaius Julius Caesar was born in July 100 BC to a noble family in the republic. As a young man, he witnessed Rome fall into chaos. The wealthy hoarded riches and the average citizens struggled to get by. Slaves were revolting as their numbers increased.

Caesar possessed many talents and a sharp wit. He was funny, charming, an excellent speaker, and commanded a strong personality. He was gifted in politics and the military.

Caesar joined the army and rose in the ranks until he became a military leader. At the time, a change in purpose was introduced to the army; instead of fighting for the good of the land, they were fighting to receive land and gold. As this practice grew, the soldiers were no longer loyal to the republic but to the generals who would pay them with substantial assets. As most of the soldiers were former peasants touched by poverty and struggle, this form of compensation was more than enough for them to switch sides.

Caesar was appointed as Governor of Spain. Not only is it a prestigious position but also lucrative one. It allowed him to pillage the locals as he saw fit. Caesar forged an alliance with two other elites, General Pompey and a wealthy patrician called Crassus, thus beginning his rise to power. The three of them created the very first Triumvirate.

When he made his way back to Rome in 60 BC, he was elected consul, one of the highest offices in the republic. However, as time passed, the Triumvirate didn't survive, as Crassus was killed on the battlefield, and Pompey made his intentions known that he wished to rule by himself without the influence of Caesar.

Caesar had a huge impact on expanding the territories of Rome. While he was busy fighting for his country in Gaul (now France), The Senate, after being influenced by Pompey, decreed that he was to return home without the protection of his army after handing them over to the new governor. They also prohibited him from running for the second consulate. These actions were made in an effort to quench Caesar's rising power.

Julius Caesar was faced with two choices: either comply with the Senate's commands and return home alone, risking his reputation and maybe his life, or start a civil war. He chose the latter. Roman law decreed that no governor was allowed to cross the Rubicon back home without being invited by the Senate. The governors were only allowed to command their armies within their assigned provinces. If the law is broken, the governor and the soldiers following him would be sentenced to death after he is stripped of his imperium.

Caesar uttered his famous words, "Alea iacta est!" meaning the dice is cast, and crossed the Rubicon with his army, ushering the start of the civil war in January of 49 BC. By 46 BC, Caesar had managed to defeat the forces of Pompey and seized Rome, declaring himself a dictator and absolute ruler. He swiftly dispatched Pompey and part of the Senate out of Rome while offering amnesties to others.

Caesar went on to reform the government. He increased the size of the Senate for better representation. He offered citizenship to many foreigners, offered veterans places to settle in new cities, and was quite charitable with some of his old foes like Marcus Junius Brutus, one of Pompey's old supporters.

7. Caesar's Gallic Wars: Conquest and Triumph

Caesar knew that in order to achieve eternal glory, one must achieve unparalleled victory in battle. The Gallic campaign is one of the most remembered political and military triumphs in Caesar's long string of victories. Caesar himself wrote down an extensive record of the Great War, though it may be wise to read the scripture with a grain of salt as it was mainly written to garner political prestige for the Roman leader.

The book he wrote included seven parts, and each part was dedicated to a year of the war.

As Caesar neared the end of his Consul in 59 BC, he was gravely compromised financially. With the help of the first Triumvirate, he managed to land the position of Governor for Cisalpine Gaul and Illyricum. Following the death of the Governor of Transalpine Gaul, he was also appointed as Governor of that province.

Following his second appointment, Caesar was approached by the Helventian tribe, a Gallic tribal confederation. The delegates wished to negotiate safe passage through the Transalpine Gaul and the land of a Roman tribe called Aedui. That migration threatened chaos in the Gual area, specifically from German warrior-like tribes that may choose to occupy the vacant Helventian territory. The Roman leader denied them passage, so they changed their route away from Roman lands entirely. To the eyes of an average beholder, this seems like a situation that has resolved itself, but alas, Caesar had other plans. He saw an opportunity to defeat the migrating tribe that would alleviate his political stature and pay off his debts from the spoils.

He gathered a sum of 24000-30000 soldiers under his command and marched in pursuit of the Helventians. He managed to catch up with them as they attempted to cross the Saone River. About a quarter were unfortunate enough not to have crossed yet because Caesar slayed them all. Negotiations resumed but were futile as Caesar's terms were steep. The fighting continued until the Romans emerged victorious, and the Helventians were ordered back to their territory, starting a seven-year-long war.

Over the seven years, Caesar suffered many losses but also had many conquests to pride himself on. He conquered the Sequani territory ruled by German tribes and the Belgae confederation. He survived an ambush from the Belgic Nervii, Atrebates, and Viromandui. Attacked and conquered Gallic tribes along the English Channel. He managed to Defeat the Venti in a memorable naval battle. Caesar had no issue with mercilessly slaughtering Germanic refugees, much to Rome's Dismay. He burned down and leveled abandoned German villages. He attempted to capture Britannia but was forced back with fierce resistance from the English. He lost some of his troops to a Belgic tribe in the northeast of the Gaul led by the Eburones, to which Caesar retaliated by slaughtering the Belgic tribes.

These events ignited the Great Gallic Revolt in 52 BC. The leadership of the revolt was in the hands of Vercingetorix following the slaughter of Romans at the hands of the Carnutes. Caesar laid siege to the city of Avaricum, where he faced off against Vercingetorix, eventually entering the city after 25 days and killing all but 800 of the original 40,000 inhabitants.

Caesar eventually managed to corner Vercingetorix in the city of Alesia, where the latter's attempts to gather reinforcements failed. He was forced to surrender to the Roman leader and later was taken to Rome to be executed in 46 BC, marking the triumphant end of the Gallic wars in favor of Rome.

8. The First Triumvirate: Crassus, Pompey, and Caesar

Caesar eventually realized that to achieve glory, you might need the assistance of others. A Triumvirate is a group of three men. This word described a secret alliance forged between three individuals to grant them more power over the Roman Political entity.

The first triumvirate was forged between Gaius Julius Caesar, Gnaeus Pompeius Magnus Aka Pompey, and Marcus Licinius Crassus in 60 BC. The alliance was forged to serve the individual ambitions of each of the men. However, it was not a match made in heaven. Two of the men, Pompey and Crassus, did not get along. This was because Pompey blatantly tried and succeeded in claiming the glory of Crassus's victory over Spartacus at Capua. Sharing the praise of his hard work did not sit well with Crassus, given that the former's contribution to the victory can be summed up in him rounding up the stragglers.

As for the relationship between Pompey and Caesar, it was a little bit more amicable. Both men favored the side of the Senate that favored the Populares in the Senate (common people) and opposed the Optimates, who only cared about maintaining their power within the wealthy elites of Rome as the traditional ruling class.

Each of the leaders had his own reasons for forming this alliance. Pompey wished to reward his veteran soldiers with land in the east but was constantly opposed by Marcus Porcius. Caesar wished to be appointed consul and reach political glory, and Crassus wished to achieve glory on the battlefield and make up for the lost funds he suffered due to the food calamity that occurred in the East.

The three men sealed their alliance by first reconciling Crassus and Pompey. To strengthen their bond further, Pompey took Caesar's daughter, Julia, for his wife.

The alliance was successful in most of its endeavors. By 59 BC, Caesar had been named co-consul with Marcus Calpurnius Bibulus, a friend of Cato. He worked hard to get Pompey the land he needed for his soldiers but was constantly vetoed by Bibulus. He then decided to take the matter into his own hands and present the proposal to the public assembly. Bibulus tried to interrupt the presentation but was thrown down the Forum steps instead and showered with garbage. Bibulus retreated from any further public appearances, which led Caesar to rule as a consul alone and grant Pompey the lands he desired. Crassus was given the chance to lead an army to cement his name as a great military leader. Unfortunately, he never achieved his dream, as he was defeated at the battle of Carrhae and decapitated by the Parthians.

9. Cleopatra and Caesar: A Fateful Alliance

Caesar came to know Cleopatra when he was pursuing Pompey out of Rome.
https://commons.wikimedia.org/wiki/File:Cleopatra_and_Caesar_by_Jean-Leon-Gerome.jpg

Caesar first came to know Cleopatra when he pursued Pompey out of Rome in 48 BC. Pompey had first fled to Greece to assemble an army to face Caesar, succeeding in gathering twice the number of soldiers Caesar had, but it was to no avail. He was still defeated in the battle of Pharsalus. He then fled to Egypt, where Caesar followed, and that's when he was enchanted by the beautiful Queen in Alexandria, both politically and emotionally. The dispute between Queen Cleopatra and her husband/brother, Ptolemy XII, disturbed the city. Ptolemy had mistakenly assumed that killing Pompey and presenting Caesar with his head would earn his favor. He was sorely mistaken. Caesar was repulsed with the gift and, as a result, seized control of the royal palace and acted as the monarch of Egypt. He commanded the royal brother and sister to disperse their armies and to settle the matter of the rightful ruler with him as their judge.

Cleopatra went to meet Caesar concealed in a carpet, as her brother's forces had blocked her from entering Alexandria. Her dramatic reveal had a much better impact on Caesar than his first meeting with her brother.

Their alliance was not built on romance and love alone; it had political aspects ingrained in it. Caesar needed Cleopatra's wealth to fund his campaign to power in Rome, and she needed his protection to secure her position as queen. His decision to declare the two siblings co-rulers again did not sit well with Ptolemy, who attempted to trap his sister with the Roman leader in the palace.

This act started a full-scale civil war in which Ptolemy was defeated in the battle of the Nile and later drowned in its namesake. Cleopatra was made Queen, and her other younger brother, Ptolemy XIV, will rule beside her. He also became her new husband despite her affair with Caesar.

Cleopatra gave birth to their son Caesarion (meaning little Caesar) shortly after. She visited Caesar in Rome a year later and stayed in one of his estates. When he was assassinated in 44 BC, she returned to Egypt, starting the tale of another affair with another Roman leader, Marc Anthony.

10. The Roman Calendar: Julius Caesar's Timeless Reform

The original dating system employed in the Republic of Rome resembled the one used in Greece, which followed the lunar cycle. It consisted of 10 months and 304 days, resulting in a 61-day gap in the winter season. In addition to continuously falling out of phase with the seasons and constantly needing correction, this lunar calendar was often exploited by the Roman officials in charge of it. They often added days to manipulate elections or extend certain political terms, abusing their authority.

In 46 BC, Caesar went to work in devising the solar calendar. He recruited Sosigenes, an astronomer from Alexandria, to aid him. Based on the solar calendar, Sosigenes calculated the year as the Egyptians do to be 365 days and a ¼. Caesar then added the missing 61 days to 46 BC, essentially moving the start of the year from March first to January first. The Julian calendar stated that the year was to be 365 days for three years in a row, followed by a year made up of 366 days (leap year). Caesar decreed that the additional day be added to February to ensure the calendar did not fall out of phase like its lunar counterpart.

Following Caesar's death, Mark Anthony renamed the month Quintilis, the 7th month of the year, to Julius (July) in honor of the fallen dictator.

11. Ides of March: Betrayal and Assassination of Julius Caesar

In Roman culture, the word Ides meant observing the full moon, which marked the 15th day and half point of every month of the Julian calendar. However, The Ides of March is a day marked in history with shame and change. By 44 BC, Caesar had appointed himself "Dictator for Life," a title that did not sit well with the powerful elite of Rome. It is argued that Caesar had sealed his fate by declaring himself as such, as Rome was known throughout history for its fight against tyrants and absolute rulers.

The conspirators behind the death of Caesar, who called themselves "The Liberators," were hung on the idea of restoring the Republic of Rome to ensure political stability.

They strongly believed that they were ridding Rome of an overly powerful tyrant. Caesar's callous ways and harsh tactics angered the aristocrats, leading them to devise a meticulous plan to end his reign.

The assassination took place in the debating chambers of the theater of Pompey, only two months after Caesar's victory over Pompey in the battle of Pharsalus.

It is believed that between 50 and 60 senators charged Caesar and stabbed him 23 times, including the two ring leaders Brutus and Cassius, whom he had considered dear companions regardless of their past allegiances with Pompey.

Cassius was unsettled by Caesar's disregard for the republican traditions and convinced Brutus, who was proud of his aristocratic heritage, to take down Caesar. Brutus held a special place in Caesar's heart as he had taken his mother, Sevilia, as a lover and considered Brutus a surrogate son. Heartbroken from the betrayal, it was said that Caesar's last famous words were "Et tu, Brute?" (You too, Brutus?). There is no way of knowing the exact words he uttered. Only those present during the betrayal could've known for sure.

Since he was stabbed so many times, it was hard to accuse any one specific person of the murder.

What the conspirators didn't see coming, though, is that following the murder of Caesar, they sealed the fate of Rome as an empire, as Caesar's adopted son Octavian later rose to power and was named Emperor Augustus.

Chapter 3: Stories of How Christianity Spread

No story of Christianity could begin without the one depicting the birth, life, and teachings of Jesus. Born in Bethlehem in Judea, Jesus belonged to the lineage of King David. The Holy Spirit aided his mother, Mary, in his conception. Mary, a young unmarried virgin, traveled with Joseph, her betrothed, to Bethlehem when they were (like many others in the region) summoned to be counted in the census. However, when they arrived, they didn't find lodging at the local inn - and were forced to spend the night in a stable. The night baby Jesus was born attracted wise men (sometimes depicted as kings, astrologers, or shepherds) who wanted to witness the product of the miraculous birth. Little is known of Jesus's childhood, but he was baptized at around 30 years old by John the Baptist.

The story of Christianity begins with the birth of Jesus.
Pasquale Paolo Cardo from Finale Ligure (Savona), Italy, CC BY 2.0
<*https://creativecommons.org/licenses/by/2.0*>, *via Wikimedia Commons.*
https://commons.wikimedia.org/wiki/File:Circello_-_The_Little_Baby_Jesus_(24169449556).jpg

It was a time of extreme religious expectations mixed with political turmoil, prompting numerous Jewish movements to be on the lookout for the prophesized Messiah who would bring much-needed changes. John the Baptist belonged to one of these movements. He was known for spreading a message of radical transformation through repentance while baptizing locals in the Jordan River. Like John, Jesus also strived to teach and preach similar agendas from an early age. When he was baptized, he took a public ministry to spread his teachings, heal and dispel demons from the possessed, and, according to some records, bring people back from the dead. Soon, he began to travel throughout Galilee, accompanied by former fishermen who followed him with their families, deserting their nets to help spread his teachings. His message emphasized the importance of turning to God and spoke about how repentance, forgiveness, love, generosity, and justice can bring one closer to the Creator. In one of his lessons, he speaks about a man who was robbed and helped by an outsider while community members left him to his luck. Having encountered many people of different backgrounds during his ministry, Jesus warned against casting judgment and counseled critics to remember their own imperfections before condemning others (referring to what is known as the commandment to love one's neighbor).

Describing it as a unique reign of justice, Jesus claimed that the Kingdom of God is closer than people think, promising liberation for the oppressed once they repent and embrace those around them. He said that the first divine Kingdom would not be built by the wealthy, powerful rulers and distinguished members of society (as is the case with earthly kingdoms) but by societal outcasts, the rejected, and the poorest. Those who heard him began to speak of Jesus as the long-promised Messiah, the redeemer of souls. They believed he was who was prophesized to turn the Kingdom of God into a reality – marking the beginning of this new faith known as Christianity. Beginning with the followers of Jesus, Christianity spread throughout the Middle East, quickly taking over the Mediterranean coast and becoming deeply ingrained in the Roman Empire.

Initially, propagators faced vicious Roman persecutions. However, despite these, due to the appealing nature of the teachings about the spirit's immortality (living after death in the Kingdom of God), Christianity grew incredibly fast. The lessons about helping the poor also contributed to the popularization of this new religion. The Apostle Paul was one of the most prominent figures to spread Christianity in Europe (and other parts of the world). During his ministry, Paul took several missionary journeys to help those in need and spread the religion among them. Paul took at least three long missionary journeys across modern-day Syria, Turkey, Greece, Cyprus, the Roman territory of Pamphylia, and others. During his travels, he disseminated Jesus' teachings and performed miracles, laying the foundations for the early Christian church.

12. Constantine the Great: The First Christian Emperor

Emperor Constantine paved the way for Rome to become a Christian empire. Born a pagan, Constantine was baptized in 312, just before launching a war campaign against his rival, Maxentius. Worried about the outcome of the war, he asked for divine guidance. Constantine received a vision in the dream about the Christian God commanding him to use a Christian symbol on his warrior's shields. Constantine obliged and overpowered Maxentius. From then on, the emperor started to express his preference for the new religion, asking his subjects to convert and providing continuous monetary support to the Christian churches. Despite this, he also continued to give money to support traditional religion. He allowed the followers of the pagan religion to build new temples and permitted sacrifices when public buildings were destroyed by lightning – although he advocated against the practice on other occasions. It was an untraditional approach (especially in the eyes of cultures that followed a monotheistic religion). Yet, by not obligating all subjects to become fixated on worship and Christian identity, Constantine ensured his good name and wasn't at risk of being overthrown (as it happened to other rules that tried to impose Christianity). Being raised in Paganism himself, Constantine found it challenging to leave the ancient religion behind. During Constantine's rule, pagans could worship as many divine figures as they wanted and in whatever form they wished. Whether this included Jesus was up to them. Some prayed to Jesus just as they did to their other gods. After he died in 337, Constantine's three sons (all raised with the Christian faith) began to use the power of the state against the followers of the pagan religion. Constantius II, for example, banned sacrifices, closed some pagan temples, and allowed bishops to convert others into Christian churches. Even with these efforts to encourage Christianity in public life, due to the vast amount of infrastructure and the unwillingness of his administrators to enforce the anti-pagan laws, Constantius couldn't extinguish paganism.

13. From Pagan to Christian: The Transformation of the Roman Empire

While missionaries like Apostle Paul and even Constantine did their best to spread Christianity in Rome, commoners had an even more considerable influence in popularizing the religion.

Libanius, a teacher from the 4th century Rome, explains that Roman pagans didn't have a unified structure, sacred books, or rituals. He says people didn't even agree on which pagan deities were authentic. In some territories across the empire, pagans worshipped gods they imagined in human form. Whereas others saw their deities as animals or inanimate objects like giant stones. Around this time, the Roman Empire had over a million structures devoted to these pagan deities. However, the gods weren't only present here. They were incorporated into people's day-today lives. They were honored on holidays, and their images adorned the Roman coins. Animals sacrificed at the temples were used for the city's meat supply.

The empire already had a mighty military and civilian administration system extending across the other territories under Roman control. The Roman citizens paid taxes to the state and were given services and protection in return. They had an incredibly efficient and dynamic administrative system coupled with a highly responsive legal institution. This required drawing upon the skills and abilities of as many citizens as possible. By the 4th century, the imperial government began to identify and draw into service the young Romans living in the provincial cities and small towns. Rosters of students were given executive positions and abundant salaries. This allowed them to obtain wealth and power provided by the imperial administrative system. Born in a small town in southern France, Libanius was among the first raised and educated to take on an administrative position. His parents supported him and saw the opportunity to make the family's name and fortune larger through him. However, the young pagan men were expected to excel and work by the emperor's rules. When they got to reap the rewards of their work, Libanius and his friends used their free time to honor their traditional religion by worshipping in the surviving pagan monuments and celebrating the old festivals. At that time, the ruler was Constantine's son, Constantius II, who didn't tolerate opposition to his regime. While Libanius and others were scared of losing the remaining of their religion, they were more afraid of endangering the wealth and prominence they'd already acquired to speak out publicly. However, this all changed when Constantius died and was superseded by his cousin Julian, a publicly declared pagan.

Due to the sudden vigorous critiques of the injustice and religious fanaticism dominating his realm, Julian made plans for a pagan restoration of the empire. Although he died soon after, his Christian successors didn't focus on the Christianization of the empire, so Libanius and other pagans could continue their ways. They praised the Christian administrative system in public, lamented the autocratic tendencies in private, and continued to collect their salaries. In other words, they continued to draw parallels and talk about both religions.

Another huge shift happened in 379 when Theodosius came to power. The new ruler frantically embraced the idea of leading Rome to a new Christian era by completely eradicating pagan practices. After restricting pagan activities, he made sacrifices punishable by death, closed pagan temples, and started punishing imperial officials who neglected to enforce his laws. This made people fearful and resulted in mass conversion. The youngest Romans born in the Theodosius-ruled Rome were all Christians. The emperor ensured that people eagerly talked about Christianity, enabling him to accelerate the rate of Christianization. Spreading Christianity through word of mouth was much more effective than using the slow administrative system.

Slowly but surely, people became disinterested in pagan worship. As a result, the buildings decayed, and the number of places of worship decreased steadily. While the statues of the pagan deities remained in public places, people started to pray to the old gods and goddesses less and less. At the beginning of the 5th century, the restrictions on pagans increased even more. Even more pagan temples were closed - until there weren't enough open to bother with efforts to shut them down. While devoted pagans traveled to rural areas, they tried to enforce their own pagan views on locals, and this didn't go well. The locals were more willing to convert to Christianity than embrace different forms of Paganism.

14. Christianity and the Rise of the Medieval Church

As one would imagine, the journey of establishing the roots of Christianity in medieval Europe wasn't smooth sailing - and not just because of the pagan resistance from barbaric countries. Around the 4th century, propagators also had to compete with a new branch of Christianity, Ariasnim. Its founder was Arius, a Roman scholar whose beliefs and teachings painted a somewhat different picture than Jesus'. Followers (which included the ranks of several Roman Emperors) of Arianism spend their days acclaiming that Jesus isn't equal to God - a notion they found much more appealing than the original version. As soon as they heard this, Germanic tribes such as the Vandals, Ostrogoths, and Visigoths adopted Arisism as well, which further complicated the expansion of the original branch throughout North Africa, the Iberian Peninsula, and Italy. Some of these tribes faced heavy persecution from the Christians.

Difficulties notwithstanding, the rise of the Medieval Church was inevitable. Soon after the earliest conquers over pagans, Arians, and alike, the Bishop of Rome was proclaimed the head of the Christian church. Although initially, not all followers accepted this event (or only embraced it partially), it marked the foundations of the Papacy and its rule over the Christian church. Once, a Roman commoner was asked what they were taught about these changes. Unfortunately, they didn't know how – or what – to answer. They only knew that the Pope (as the Bishop of Rome was known across the empire) had considerable influence. They also said they were afraid of what the changes would bring because it was rumored that the Papacy was overseen and controlled by the Byzantine Empire. This was in the early medieval period. When commoners were asked the same question a couple of centuries later, they knew that the Pope's mission was to convert major parts of Western Europe and were less apprehensive about the possibility of accepting the Papacy as a supreme power. Gradually, the Roman church not only grew but separated from their co-religions in the Eastern Mediterranean. By the time the Middle Ages were in full swing, the main churches would be known as Roman Catholic and Orthodox.

15. St. Patrick and the Spread of Christianity in Ireland

St. Patrick is a well-known figure in European history and Christianity. He is credited with the religion's dissemination in Ireland and later other parts of Europe. Born in Britain in 386, St. Patrick became enslaved and sold by pirates to an Irish farm, where he spent his days working and praying. This routine shaped his mindset and even showed him the road to escape slavery. Legend has it that St. Patrick had a vivid dream telling him to go to a boat that would take him home. Being a Christian man of faith, he immediately thought it was God who spoke to him and did as was told, successfully escaping to France in 408 A.D. After a short stay in France, he found his way to his family in Britain. Here, he was ordained as a bishop in 432 A.D. and tasked with spreading Christianity by Pope Celestine I.

St. Patrick is a well-known figure in European history.

Soon after, St. Patrick had yet another dream. This one depicted the Irish begging him to visit Ireland and assist the newly converted Christians in the country. He saw Irish people burdened by tribal warfare, slavery, and pagan traditions. Not wanting to let down those in need, he immediately traveled to Ireland, where, besides helping Christians, he also began to introduce the religion to the Irish pagans. To fight the resistance toward the new religion, he had the ingenious idea to incorporate pagan rituals into Christian practices.

While in Ireland, St. Patrick was attacked and captured several times by the Irish pagan tribes. However, he would always surrender willingly, as he saw the opportunity to teach his faith to his capturers. Due to his deep reverence for love, forgiveness, hard work, and social grace, he often successfully converted entire pagan tribes to Christianity. This led to the infamous saying that he drove the snakes out of Ireland (referring to the pagans).

16. The Age of Conversion: Christianizing the Barbarian Kingdoms

Despite a rough start, Christian missionaries sent from both Ireland and the Papacy were able to convert numerous rulers of European countries by the 7th century. However, the barbaric kingdoms became increasingly hard to approach after the Vikings invaded and established their rule during the 8th and 10th centuries. Thankfully, they had the support of now-Christian emperors such as Charlemagne (the Carolingian emperor), who launched a series of passionate campaigns against the Germanic tribe known as the Saxons. After a three-year invasion and destruction of numerous holy sites, the Saxons surrendered and converted to Christianity. Similar to him, Norway's Olaf Tryggvason also attempted to convert his subjects. However, his attempts were far less successful, and he was overthrown. This was around the 8th century when the majority of Norse people said, "We will never abandon the ancient religion!" Some were more resistant than others. In 1000 AD, a representative of the Alîing (the Icelandic people's general assembly), Thorgeir Thorkelsson, was given the responsibility of deciding in 1000 whether the people of Iceland would follow Christianity or the Norse religion. He spent an entire day and the following night mulling over the issue before finally settling on the conversion. Other Scandinavian countries were also fully converted by the 11th century. By contrast, it took until after the darkest period of the Middle Ages for the Sami people of Northern Scandinavia to bow down to baptism.

During the 9th century, both the Byzantine church and the Papacy targeted the Bulgarians as the next nation to bring under their jurisdiction. However, they had to contend with the Bulgarian ruler, Boris's unusual defense strategy. Since the two sides had different interests, Boris pretended to seek an alliance with both. He was patient in determining which option would best serve his own strategic goals. He eventually came to an agreement with the Byzantine Empire, leading to the establishment of the national Bulgarian church. The astute Bulgarians created the formal liturgy for their church using their own language and beliefs. Only a century later, Mieszko I, the first ruler of the neighboring Poland, embraced Christianity. According to legend, he was pressured into baptism by his wife, who was of Bohemian origins. I went to Boleslav I, Duke of Bohemia, Mieszko's wife's father, who was already a Christian, and asked for his loyalty. His wife told him that her father would probably support him if he converted. During the same period, the Byzantine Empire attempted to evangelize populations in other Eastern European regions, including what is now Russia and Ukraine. It was just as lagging here as it was in Scandinavia to convert. Christianity didn't become a generally accepted religion in the area until Vladimir the Great, the ruler of Kievan Rus, at the turn of the millennium. Vladimir convened with adherents of many faiths in 986, including Jews, Muslims, and Christians, before selecting his own religion to enforce upon his subjects. After learning about the culture in Constantinople (the capital of the Byzantine Empire), Vladimir and his family were baptized and embraced the teachings of the Orthodox Church.

The Hungarian ruler, King Stephen I, also embraced Christianity at the beginning of the 11th century. While initially resistant, his people followed his example of getting baptized and leaving their pagan religion behind. This took considerable effort, but everyone became more agreeable to the new faith once things were on their way. They praised Stephen I for building churches and were ready to conflict punishment on those who didn't follow Christian practices.

Being the last crucial holdouts to Christianity in Europe, the Baltic region was only fully conquered in the 14 century. This marked the end of the crusade that started in the mid-12th century and was plagued by the darkest period of the Middle Ages. The unconquered Grand Duchy of Lithuania was still a crucial regional power in the mid-14th century. However, at the end of the century, the ruling Grand Duke married the Polish Queen and was baptized as a Roman Catholic Christian based on his wife's wishes. A year later, he imposed Christianity on the Lithuanian people, although elements of their pagan faith survived past this period.

Chapter 4: Viking Expeditions and Their Stories

Originating from Scandinavia, the Vikings were mysterious Norsemen who, through their many expeditions across Europe from 750-1050 C.E., had a monumental impact on the continent's history. The Vikings were known for their exceptional sailing and navigational skills, which allowed them to travel, explore, and conquer sight far from their homeland. It's still unclear what prompted them to undertake their journeys. Historians suggest population pressure, trade, and the pursuit of wealth and prestige. This chapter explores how their journeys affected the cultures they met with and the lasting influence of Viking expeditions on European history.

The Vikings were known for their exceptional sailing and navigational skills.
U+1F360, CC BY-SA 4.0 <https://creativecommons.org/licenses/by-sa/4.0>, via Wikimedia Commons. https://commons.wikimedia.org/wiki/File:Vikings_Undead.jpg

17. Trade and Raids: The Dual Face of Viking Expeditions

At first, Vikings thrived in their agricultural and rural society, with most clan members working as farmers and fishermen. While the fishermen would always return home with full nets, the farmers were more and more often left without a good harvest. Due to the harsh climate conditions in Scandinavia, the soil wasn't overly fertile. As their population expanded, after a while, there wasn't enough grain to keep everyone fed during the long and icy winters. As food shortages became a regular occurrence, some chieftains decided to take what their tribe needed from other tribes, marking the beginning of the Viking raids. At first, the attacks only occurred across local territories, but soon enough, they began to spread across Europe, too. As they started to expand their horizons, the Vikings found many thriving cities on the coastal area of the continent, along with monasteries – which turned out to be easy targets due to their isolation and defenseless inhabitants.

When they started to venture beyond Western Europe, the Vikings slowly began settling, trading, and farming in their new homelands. Journeying across the North Atlantic and through the icy rivers to Constantinople, they reached North America at the beginning of the 11th century (over 400 years before Columbus). While their colony here was short-lived, their settlements in other parts of Europe thrived beyond imagination. Their voyages, accompanied by a reign of terror, soon became history. Some tribes, not all, even started to embrace Christianity (albeit very slowly), which meant they ceased raiding monasteries. The favorable climate outside Scandinavia also made farming more feasible, so there was no need to continue the sea-faring warrior lifestyle.

As the Vikings gradually embraced trade and settlement, they were driven by the same goals as they were during their raids. They were after wealth, even if this meant obtaining fertile agricultural land. Naturally, they had to interact with the locals, which was often a hit or miss. In England, for example, they started coming with the Britons, even embracing the hybridization of their cultures. Meanwhile, the Vikings kept to themselves in Russia and Normandy, remaining a minority – although they did their best to blend their culture and respect the locals. All across Europe, the Vikings traded weapons, tools, soap, jewelry, cooking vessels, and building materials. Wherever they started bartering, they established enormous commercial centers, reviving small, dying markets and areas - much to the local population's happiness and benefit.

18. The Sacking of Lindisfarne: The Dawn of the Viking Age

The Vikings first attacked a monastery looking for loot at Lindisfarne in 793 A.D. The Vikings' killing and enslaving of defenseless monks caused outrage - but the symbolic defeat was even more prominent. Medieval Christians considered Lindisfarne one of the birthplaces of Christianity in Britain. They viewed the sacking of this site as a desecration of the Creator's sanctuary and shedding the blood of monks akin to dispersing waste across the streets. In a letter to Higbald (the bishop of Lindisfarne at the time), a priest named Alcuin claimed that the attack was God's punishment for the monks of Lindisfarne. He was sure the lamentable event was a sign of some terrible mistake. Since he didn't know what the sin was, Alcuin advised the surviving monks to avoid drinking ale, wearing fancy clothes, and other "frivolous" behavior, pray even more often than usual, and fortify their faith in God. He also prompted the relocation of the surviving relics and artifacts (like St. Cuthbert's body) to another, less accessible location.

According to another record of the event, people saw dragons flying across the sky above Lindisfarne before the attack. The woefully terrified locals claimed to see fiery dragons sail the sky, letting out immense sheets of burning light. They even tied the great famine that soon followed to this event, along with heathen men wreaking havoc in the church of God on Holy Island (referring to the Viking raid of Lindisfarne). However, none of them could've imagined that the sacking of Lindisfarne was only the beginning of the Viking's reign of terror in Britain. Through the following years, the Vikings led entire armies into Britain, making significant conquests along the way.

19. The Vikings in Russia: The Rus' Legacy

Britain was only their first target when the Vikings started spreading from Scandinavia. As they began to head east, along the Dnieper and Volga rivers, they saw the opportunity to take control of trade routes that enabled them to reach the mighty Byzantine Empire. Lured by trade opportunities and wealth, they advanced to Constantinople. From the

9th century onwards, these Vikings spreading toward the west became known as the Rus (or Varangians). They conquered the territories of modern-day Russia, Ukraine, and Belarus. Establishing a ruling point in Kyiv in 840, they were named the Kievan Rus. According to the Russian Primary Chronicle (a historical account of the region compiled in the 12th century by Kievan monks), the rule over their territory was initially divided between three brothers. Truvor established a base in Izborsk, Sineus, at Beloozero, while the third brother, Rurik, lived at Novgorod. The latter became known as the capital of the land of the Rus (the original form of the name "Russia"). After their death, Ririk claimed his brother's territory, making Novgorod the capital of the entire domain of the Rus. His successor, Oleg, relocated the capital to Kyiv. True to his Viking ancestors, Oleg continued to conquer new territories, increasing the rule of Kievan Rus and amassing incredible wealth through lucrative trade with Constantinople.

According to legends, a prophecy foretold Oleg that he would die riding one of his horses. To avoid this, Oleg stopped riding that animal. However, after successfully expanding his territory (and thinking himself invincible), Oleg began to consider riding the horse once again – only to discover that it had died. He did, however, find its bones. Satisfied that it would never cause his demise now, Oleg stomped on the animal's skull. Just at that moment, a snake shot from underneath the animal's bones and bit him. Oleg died soon after.

Oleg's successor was Rurik's son, Igor, who, like his predecessor, set out to conquer and trade. Unfortunately, he wasn't good at collecting bounty from the conquered territories, and the tribes rebelled against the high prices, killing him. He was succeeded by his wife Olga, who, according to the stories, took revenge on her husband's killers. When the emissaries (belonging to the tribes her husband wanted to conquer) went to see her, Olga made them believe that she would marry one of them – only to trick them into being burned alive in her bathhouse.

When Vladimir the Great assumed rule and embraced Christianity, the era of the Kievan Rus started to come to an end. Besides agreeing to convert to Christianity, Vladimir also sent the emperor of the Byzantine Empire 6,000 soldiers to defend his throne. He was allowed to marry the emperor's sister in exchange, forging a powerful alliance between the two domains. As a result of this deal, the Kievan Rus began to embrace the Byzantine culture. Vladimir erected churches to encourage people to practice the new faith, even building schools to improve literacy (adding to the spread of Christianity). While the economy flourished and Kievan Rus continued to expand, after the rule of Vladimir's son Yaroslav I, the federation fell victim to royal power struggles. Further instability was caused by the Crusades, and by the time the Mongols invaded the territory in the 13th century, the Kievan Rus stood no chance of fighting back.

20. The Viking Siege of Paris: A City Under Threat

France's (known as the Frankish Empire at the time) first encounter with Viking raiders in 799 marked the beginning of an extended period of raids of the territory. However, it wasn't the most memorable of the Viking attacks – even though the empire had plenty of time to prepare its future defense strategy. In 810, Emperor Charlemagne established an early defense system of watchtowers and coastal forts across the northern coast. To fortify its response to the threat posed by Viking raids, the defense system was backed up by a sizable establishment of a naval fleet that would patrol along the coastline. Although this didn't stop the Vikings from continuing their reign of terror across the Frankish Empire, the defense system did stop their attack at the mouth of the river Seine.

Unfortunately, two and half decades later, the defense system failed when Danish Vikings in Frisia and Dorestad broke through, commencing a systematic raid pattern in the religion. These raids had political motivations. Rather than continuing their sporadic attacks, Vikings began to plan and coordinate their strategies, leading them to more sizable bounties and minimal losses. It also involved setting up permanent bases in the conquered areas, leading to the establishment of early Viking settlements. Moreover, the raids across the Frankish Empire were often the result of power struggles among Scandinavian Vikings. Tribe leaders wanted to expand their territories and gain more power to establish dominance over rival tribes.

The chieftains accumulated wealth and status, and the spoils were distributed among the raider warriors. Naturally, the most successful warriors got them, which led to fierce competition among the leaders. Historians theorize that this was behind the sudden shift in tactics toward more organized raiding.

As the raids grew more frequent and brutal, they caused widespread panic among the locals. When the Viking settlements started growing in number, it threatened to destabilize the Frankish Empire. The reason was simple: the newly established settlements served as excellent bases for attacks and could serve as bases for further Viking attacks.

Amid all this chaos, the Vikings arrived in Paris in 1845, immediately launching an attack by entering the city, pillaging, and causing destruction on their way. Led by Reginherus, thousands of Viking warriors arrived in the Seine on 120 ships, quickly powering through the Frankish defense made from a smaller army put together by King Charles in haste. Even a short-lived plague outbreak in their camp didn't stop the Vikings from plundering and occupying the city.

Charles made further attempts to push back the invasion but to no avail. When he realized he couldn't overpower the Vikings, he decided to pay them a ransom of 7,000 livres of gold and silver – asking them to withdraw their forces in return. While the substantial amount of precious metal was well received by the Vikings, they only viewed it as compensation for earlier defeats (they lost lands and settlements to Charles's army earlier). More payments followed in an attempt to buy time and make peace with the Vikings in the future. The payments are known as Danegeld, although it's unclear whether this term was used at the time. Charles was heavily criticized for paying the ransom, but he also had to deal with local revolts across his reign, pressures from other European rulers, and even disputes with his brothers. Paying off the Vikings was a prudent move to avoid further conflict and take at least one burden off the shoulders of the Frankish Empire.

While the Vikings eventually withdrew from the city, the Siege of Paris in 845 was a pivotal point in the European past. It brought forth the dangers of a clash between two very different cultures. Moreover, the Vikings forever carved their name into history by triumphing over the Franks. While the invasion wasn't a complete success, it left its mark on the entire continent, and according to some, its effect can still be felt (even if only in France). Even more importantly, the tribes continued to loot along the coast while traveling back to their home settlements. Their expansion into the empire continued, and they were able to demonstrate their military prowess many times over in the future. For the Franks, the defeat exposed their vulnerability to enemy attacks.

21. The Danelaw: Vikings in England

After the attack on Lindisfarne, The Vikings continued their raids on the country's northeast coast. They ransacked other monasteries, heralding the 300-year-long Viking age England (and the rest of Europe) was about to endure. The Vikings continued to loot on Irish, Scottish, and Irish soil in the following years. Eventually, they grew tired of moving around to raid and started conquering usable lands. The most notable invasion was led by Ivar the Boneless and Halfdan Ragnarsson (both sons of Ragnar). After amassing an immense force of the Great Heathen Army (as it was called by the famous Anglo-Saxon Chronicle), the Vikings were ready to conquer. Besides wanting to settle, Ragnar's sons were also led by revenge for their father's death. According to the Norse sagas, the King of Northumbria is said to have slain Ragnar by plunging him into a pit filled with poisonous snakes.

England was split into four kingdoms upon the arrival of the Viking army, namely Wessex, East Anglia, Mercia, and Northumbria. East Anglia's ruler quickly bargained with the Vikings to rescue himself and his followers. Therefore, the invasion didn't continue long there. In return for sparing his kingdom and subjects, the king provided the warriors with his best horses to continue their campaign. Shortly after, the Vikings conquered York, the capital of Northumbria, and the rothers were able to take their revenge on its king. In his place, they put a ruler they could manage, and they led their army forward in search of more territory.

After a decade of conflict, only the kingdom of Wessex remained unconquered. It was ruled by Alfred the Great, who, after encountering the Danish warlord and Viking leader Guthrum at the Battle of Edington, claimed a victory against the barbarians. This led to a temporary peace agreement between the Vikings and the kingdom of Wessex. Known as the Treaty of Wedmore, the consensus prompted Guthrum to embrace Christianity (and undergo baptism) and Alfred to become his godfather. Guntrum was also to withdraw his army from the kingdom. Soon after, Guthrum and Alfred came to another agreement that outlined their respective domains and trading possibilities in detail, guaranteeing a more durable peace.

Following the new agreement, Viking laws and customs extended throughout the kingdom, reaching the northern boundaries, the Midlands, and London on the southern side. The name of this region was identified as Danelaw, derived from the Old English term Dena lagu, meaning "Danes' law."

The Danelaw region.
Hel-hama, CC BY-SA 3.0 <https://creativecommons.org/licenses/by-sa/3.0>, via Wikimedia Commons: https://commons.wikimedia.org/wiki/File:England_878.svg

While the Vikings didn't have colonies across this entire area, they had bases in five critical points in the east. These were Lincoln, Leicester, Derby, Nottingham and Stamford. These were initially just the outposts of five Viking armies that had invaded and established themselves in the region. As they developed into towns, they were dubbed the Five Boroughs and were governed by Viking Jarls. Even though they operated separately, all of them were clearly under the direct authority of the Yorkist kings.

The Anglo-Saxons and the Vikings coexisted for many decades after that, trading, blending together, and creating mixed communities. The language and place names of the Danelaw that have persisted to this day show the most obvious effects of their coexistence. For instance, the Old Norse word for "village" was the source of the suffix -by, frequently used at the end of Viking settlement names (like Derby, for example). Other Viking place names begin with 'sky' or 'skin.' Modern Britons even have the Vikings to thank for the words "law" and "wrong," none of which existed in Old English. They were all incorporated into English after establishing a legal system in Danelaw.

Unfortunately, peace could only last for so long. After almost a century, conflicts began to arise between the Vikings and their neighbors once again. By this time, Alfred took advantage of the peace agreements to reinforce his army and erect numerous forts for better defense against the Vikings. He was succeeded by his eldest daughter, Æthelflæd, who heroically led the fight against the barbarians. She began by taking over the rule of the kingdom of Mercia, where she found the resources she needed to launch an offensive strategy against the Vikings. This move played a significant role in Danelaw's conquest. By 954 A.D., the Five Boroughs had fallen, and Eric Bloodaxe, the most brutal Viking and current King of Northumbria, was displaced from the region. This marked the end of Danelaw in England.

Despite Danelaw's eradication in England, the Vikings were very active on English soil. While they seemingly ceased their raids and retreated to other settlements, they would return. They marched for the English cities shortly after gathering their armies, and less than a century later, they had already triumphantly taken over the nation. Sweyn Forkbeard became the first Danish king of England in 1013. Cnut the Great, his son, succeeded him until he died in 1035. The last Viking monarch, Harald Hardrada of Norway, was not vanquished until the English army under monarch Harold's command won the Battle of Stamford Bridge in 1066.

In the same way, their culture left a permanent legacy across the European continent (and beyond). Viking traditions persisted in the region of former Danelaw long after the warriors suffered their last defeat. The decades of coexistence left its trace in the local population, whose DNA is still heavily laced with Scandinavian roots.

Chapter 5: Stories of a Black Death Most Deadly

Following the sudden spread of the most recent pandemic, Covid-19, people have since started looking back on historic milestones that may resemble the heart-wrenching effects of this unfortunate outbreak. One of the most unforgettable tragedies in human history that involves pestilence is the Black Death. It's also known as the Great Mortality in reference to the highest fatality rate caused in history (historic documentation of estimated fatalities has varied significantly between 25–200 million deaths), which amounted to about a third of the population.

The behemoth that is the Black Death was a threat the European continent did not see coming prior to the 14th century. The infamous plague is guilty of reaping more lives than any war or illness has ever done before it. It is a popular belief that modern-day epidemics originated from the medieval period, making this a disease that's been passed down through generations in different forms.

The behemoth that is the Black Death was a threat to the European continent.
https://commons.wikimedia.org/wiki/File:Doutielt3.jpg

Origins of the Black Death

The Black Death originally made its presence known in the inner parts of Asia and China. It left its footprint on the Mongol warriors of Kipchak Khan Janibeg when he attempted to lay siege to the Genoese port of Kaffa in Crimea (known today as Feodosiya) in 1347. The plague did not deter him from his quest; instead, he harnessed it as a Bioweapon using trebuchets to catapult his infected, deceased soldiers into the town of Kaffa, hoping they would infect the town's people.

As a result of Janibeg's inhumane tactics, the Black Death was carried by Genoesian ships from the Black Sea that were westbound. They delivered it to the Mediterranean ports (Messina, Italy), effectively inflicting the horrors of the pestilence on western Eurasia and North Africa for the following few years.

Giovanni Boccaccio painted a morbid picture of the Black Plague in the Decameron. He said, "A great many breathed their last in the public streets, day and night; a large number perished in their homes, and it was only by the stench of their decaying bodies that they proclaimed their death to their neighbors. Everywhere, the city was teeming with corpses."

By 1350, the Black Plague had made its way all across Europe, reaching the North, including England, Scotland, Scandinavia, and the Baltic countries.

While many historians argue that the plague was exterminated by 1353, evidence supports its recurrence several times from 1360 to 1400. It is thought to have arrived in Europe in waves from central Asia through scores of rodents affected by climate change and infested with plague-carrying fleas.

Modern researchers conclude that the disease was caused by bacillus bacteria called Yersinia Pestis. This bacterium is believed to have traveled not only on the backs of rodents but also through humans, hibernating in lice, biding their time to wreak havoc on Medieval Europe. Researchers believe that the Black Death consisted of three plagues. Bubonic, Pneumonic, and Septicemic. The one believed to have infiltrated Europe the most in the 14th century is the Bubonic Plague, with symptoms that included swelling in Lymph Nodes (specifically around the armpits and groin), creating sores that then turn into black scabs, hence the name Black Plague. It also caused a running fever and joint pain. This type was often responsible for 30-75% of deaths of the total people afflicted by it if it was left untreated within the first 72 hours. You might think this type of plague is catastrophic; however, the other two types - Pneumonic and Septicemic plagues — were fatal to all infected.

The Black Death's Impact

While the physical damage this disease caused to the population at the time was cataclysmic, it had other unpleasant effects that reshaped the continent for quite some time. This disease left its fingerprints on the economy, religious institutions, politics, and societal conditions. Each of these stories depicts the cruelty of some humans when faced with traumatic events.

22. Flagellants and Fanatics: Religious Responses to the Black Death

When people were first privy to the Black Death, they treated their dead with as much respect as ever. The mourners would assemble coffins and go through the traditional burial rituals of their loved ones. However, as it became clear that this disease was more vicious than anyone had ever thought and was here to stay for a while, people grew desperate, and the officials declared that the dead would be buried in mass graves due to the huge number of corpses, and lack of space for singular plots.

Due to a shortage of land, Pope Clement VI went as far as consecrating the Rhone River so they could get rid of the corpses in it.

The peasants who witnessed the calamity that was happening were mortified. They believed that the plague was a result of the wrath of God. Their beliefs were backed by the declaration from the Roman Catholic Church, which also asserted this belief. They beseeched the citizens to pray and made a point of organizing religious marches to ask God to spare them from the disease. Nonetheless, even through all of these religious efforts, doubts started seeping through people's minds as they saw their religious figures (Monks, Nuns, and Friars) dying as easily as the rest of them. In some places, the religious services and sermons stopped because no one was around to lead them.

People started to find refuge in magic, protective talismans, and spells. Others burned incense, thinking that the stench of the dead was the reason for the illness. Many more thought they could chase the disease away with cannon fire and church bells.

These unfortunate circumstances paved the way for the birth of the Flagellant Movement. The movement consisted of a group of penitents that traveled together from one place to another while whipping themselves in an effort to atone for their sins. These motions originated in Austria and later picked up momentum in Germany and France. Those fanatics, who were often led by self-proclaimed masters with no religious credibility whatsoever, had a major hand in spreading the plague further. They also caused havoc in societies when they made it a habit to attack minorities like the Jews. The faith in the church started to diminish as a direct result of the scandals and the shameful conduct and thriftless attitude of clergy, leading people to believe that the plague was a result of the paranormal.

23. Scapegoats in Crisis: Persecution of Jews During the Black Death

Fear was the strongest catalyst of this prejudice and aggression. One of the most unfortunate consequences of the Black Plague was the containment of Jewish society. Christian believers attributed the disease to Jewish magic, believing that the Jews had deliberately poisoned the wells to harm the Christians using black magic. As more people lost faith in the church and started to look for supernatural explanations, many directed that unneeded attention to the Jewish community, including the fanatics of the Flagellant Movement.

Some Jews were coerced into confessing through torture, and later, around 20 Jews were murdered. King Peter of Aragon made an effort to dial down the hostilities against the Jewish community; however, that didn't stop the riots that broke out across Europe against them, forcing several monarchs to issue orders for their arrest.

This mania spread like wildfire to communities that hadn't yet been touched by the plague. In Chillon, not far from Geneva, the Jews were attacked four months before any of the locals fell ill. This was triggered by the well-poisoning rumor that spread from afflicted areas.

A lot of the crimes committed against the Jews happened in areas that spoke mainly German; however, it is thought to have originated in French and Spanish territories. Some historians argue that there was no direct relation between the massacres and the occurrence of the disease, while others claim that the burning of Jews started before the disease made its way to Europe. In other tales, the Christian governments were to blame for what was believed to be a meticulous plan executed to target the Jews.

There were two prevailing theories to explain the injustice the Jews suffered from. The scapegoating effect and the complementariness effect. The scapegoating effect was a result of the downward slope the illness was taking, leading people to blame the marginalized group in society for it (not unlike how Asians were targeted and blamed for Covid-19 in 2020). The complementary effect was due to the huge impact the Jews had on the economy, making the roles they filled more integral as the Plague hit.

Anti-Semitism spread almost as fast as the Plague by the wealthy and powerful who were indebted to the Jews (later referred to as Jew Killers) in an effort to absolve themselves of their debts.

At the start of the Black Death, it was estimated that Jewish communities were present in around 363 cities. By the end of the Pestilence, it is believed that almost half of these communities were either exterminated or forced to leave their homes.

24. Social Upheaval: The Peasants' Revolt and the Plague

The Black Plague significantly impacted the social status quo, taking Medieval Europe by storm. In England, a significant shortage of laborers and peasants occurred, and an estimated 40% of its population perished from the Plague (the height of such loss was between the summer of 1348 and the spring of 1350). Being an agricultural nation that depended on the abundance of lower-class workers at the time, this caused quite a crisis, specifically for the upper-class citizens of the society. When the workers realized a higher demand for their skills, they started to bargain with their masters for better wages. They abandoned their villages in search of higher pay in exchange for their services. These acts caused a great deal of dismay among the upper classes, who, until the Plague had hit, enjoyed luxuries and privileges that the peasants only witnessed from afar.

After a lot of pressure from the lords of the lands on the government, the statute of laborers was passed with the blessing of King Edward III.

The law entailed that the peasants and workers were not to take advantage of the shortage of laborers and ask for extra wages but were forced to work in exchange for the same wages they had accepted before the Black Plague. These wages were to be determined by the people who hired them. A new tax poll was forced on all peasants (men and women) regardless of their wealth.

This caused an uproar in the lower classes not only because it limited their income but because of the events that followed.

People who tried to flee their homes seeking better pay were dragged back by force by the landlords. Any workers who refused to abide by the law would expect physical penalties and hefty fines from the local lords. Some of the landowners tried to turn people into serfs or villeins (old-fashioned tenants who paid their dues to the landlords through service in return for land) to save money by not paying wages.

These evil and unjust acts were the fuel that lit the peasant revolt, also known as the great revolt. The lower class endured for 30 years following the law's decree until they marched from their villages to London in May of 1381. The Christian values that all men are born equal and should be treated with respect were used by the revolters to back up the campaign. On the other hand, the institution of the Medieval Church was condemned for many of the society's shortcomings.

The commoners rose against the old shackles that entailed that people who were born in privilege were above them and deserved more. A chant was repeated: "When Adam delved and Eve span, who then was the gentleman." It expressed their rage at being treated with inequality. They burned down buildings and set prisoners free. Sheriffs and officials were taken and killed. Manors were torched, burning most of the records at Maidstone, Canterbury, and Rochester in an effort to destroy the seignorialism.

As the villagers arrived in London on June 13th, they were met with more disgruntled commoners who had their own feuds with the rich in the city. A lot of the lawyers and crown officials were targeted as a result of old grievances and grudges. On June 14th, King Richard II, believed to have only been 14 at the time, left the safety of the London Tower to meet with the peasants and hear their demands at Mile End. The King listened to the demands recited to him by the leader of the peasants, Wat Tyler of Maidstone (he was believed to have been accompanied by another leader, the demagogue Priest John Ball). Richard agreed to the demands and even allowed the peasants to exact vengeance on whomever they thought deserved it.

Following this meeting, the London Tower was stormed, and the Archbishop of Canterbury, Simon Sudbury, was captured and executed by a mob led by Johanna Ferrour.

The looting and murder continued for another day, causing the King to call for another meeting with the rebel's leader on June 15th, this time in a field in Smithfield outside of London. The demands made in this meeting included:

- The complete abolition of Serfdom and villeins
- All to receive free fishing and hunting rights
- A retraction of the labor law that limited increases in wages
- The church riches are to be redistributed, specifically that of great abbeys
- The participation of peasants in the government
- The only authority should be in the hands of the crown and not delegated to the landlords

The remainder of the meeting is shrouded in mystery. Some say that Tyler was agitated and seemed to have intended to strike the King; some say he spat water at the King's feet. As a result, either William

Walworth, the Mayor of London, or a soldier of the King's guard stepped up and stabbed him. It is said that he fled the meeting and managed to be taken to a hospital for treatment, only to be brought back to Smithfield to be executed. The King declared to the crowd that their demands shall be met. He stated that he is their leader and that they should go home as they have fulfilled their quest. Many peasants heeded his words and returned to their lands; however, the King did not intend to keep his word.

Instead of honoring his promise, King Richard went out of his way to round up almost 150 of the rebels and execute them by hanging. There were smaller attempts for rebellion after that, which were ruthlessly annihilated, and their ring leaders executed as traitors, including John Ball, who wasn't only hanged but dismembered as well.

Tyler's head was put on display on the London Bridge.

As disappointing as this outcome was, following the King's short imprisonment and unexplained death, some reforms started to blossom in England. The poll tax was revoked, and the limitations placed on wages were not as strictly enforced, while villains could buy their freedom from their landlords. The laws no longer served to condemn the peasants to servitude but to document that the laborer had indeed bought their freedom and that the land was theirs to pass down to their lineage.

25. A Blow to Feudalism: Economic Impacts of the Black Death

Not unlike what we're experiencing today in the aftermath of Covid-19, the economy following the spread of the Black Plague was extremely inflated. The disease made it difficult and unsafe to acquire or manufacture products due to quarantine and fear of infection, so the prices for local and foreign goods went through the roof. Many households who have lost their breadwinners were dependent on charities to sustain them, which put a strain on the civic entities of the governments.

While the peasants' revolt did not conclude in a positive resolution for the economic status of the lower class, in the long run, things seemed to look up a bit. With the gradual fading of serfs, workers no longer had to man any one land, and they were free to roam and find better compensation for their work, reshaping the face of the agrarian economy. Due to the scarcity of workers following the death toll of the Black Death, if one were to leave a lord, another would hire them immediately. The standards of living were ultimately raised all around. Per capita incomes and wages started to grow. With the increase of wealth for the lower class came the ability to buy more products, which increased the production of the demanded goods. The economic position of Europe following the plague was altered drastically in comparison to other continents like Asia.

26. Surviving the Plague: Stories of Resistance and Resilience

The stories of the Black Death are not all tales of despair and societal melancholy. Some stories inspire resilience, recovery, and courage in facing the unknown. Look at the cultural response to the Pestilence's arrival in Europe. You'll notice that it varied between finding purpose in the face of horrific circumstances through spiritual enlightenment and salvation in the afterlife or through fighting for justice and liberation. These themes were heavily emphasized in the 14th century.

Evidence of resilience can be found in artistic expressions observed in literature like The Decameron, written by Giovanni Boccaccio, or The Canterbury Tales by Geoffrey Chaucer, inspired during the Plague. It also affected the art world as a wide collection of paintings was produced during the Black Death.

Now, it is true that the Plague had a deadly immediate touch on the economy. In hindsight, though, the way communities seemed to bounce back, pick up the pieces, and reassemble the societal structure in a better and just manner is proof of how the people afflicted by the tragedy adapted to the changes promptly and efficiently.

One of the most debated theories in history is the "light touch" of the Plague in the southern areas of Europe. This story mainly focuses on the southern Netherlands, which was deemed fictitious. It suggested that the lower countries were not as affected by the Black Death as the rest of Europe; however, it does shed light on the ease with which these areas managed to recover their population. As it turns out, some believe that this was due to the resilient urban settlements allowing migrants from devastated rural areas to take refuge in their lands.

Chapter 6: Renaissance Stories

The Renaissance is a pivotal era in European history that is characterized by the rise of distinguished families who transformed the cultural and political landscape of the region. This chapter explores the tales of influential families that shaped the Italian Renaissance. You will learn about their political, cultural, and economic power and influence.

The Renaissance is a pivotal era in European history that is characterized by the rise of the cultural and political landscape.

https://commons.wikimedia.org/wiki/File:Last_Judgement_by_Michelangelo.jpg

Italy was organized into several city-states, such as Siena, Florence, Venice, and Naples, at the time the Medicis rose to power. The Medicis attained power in Florence in 1434, where the Renaissance started, and ruled for over six decades. Wealthy families in this affluent, cultural place could afford to support rising artists, a movement the Medici family supported.

The Medici are among the most influential families in European history. They established Florence as a cultural hub, transformed the banking industry, made political reforms, and were patrons of the arts, giving rise to the High Renaissance, which was a period of flourishing artistic endeavors.

27. Advancements in Banking and Finance

Cosimo the Elder built the Medici bank in Florence, which later branched across other city-states and even foreign cities like Bruges and London. The branches he opened in the neighboring countries allowed the Papacy to order goods from outside Italy.

The strategic locations of the branches, alongside their invention of transformative financial tools, made them pioneers in the banking industry. For instance, they introduced the double-entry bookkeeping system, now considered a basic and fundamental finance and accounting principle. Transcontinental payments were risky at the time, which was a problem that the Medicis took care of by inventing the Letters of Credit, which serve as proof of payment yet to be received.

Patronage and Artistic Flourish

The Medici family helped establish some of the most popular Italian landmarks, including St. Peter's Basilica, the Sistine Chapel, and the Duomo of Florence, through their patronage, relationships, and political strategies. Florence didn't have the strongest military force compared to other Italian city-states, making it vulnerable to attacks. The fact that the Medicis were skilled diplomats significantly helped their position.

Cosimo the Elder brilliantly negotiated his way through a series of wars in Lombardy, ending them because he knew that the clash would hurt trade procedures. He was able to help all the states come to an agreement regarding mutual territory, which Lorenzo de' Medici, his successor, kept alive. Lorenzo was loved by the people because he freed slaves and performed other similar kind acts.

Some suggest that Botticelli's Pallas and the Centaur was made in honor of Lorenzo, as his negotiation skills also protected Florence and its independence against cities with strong armies. Lorenzo embodied Pallas Athena's wisdom, and Naples portrayed humanity's fertility, which is symbolized by the centaur. Lorenzo was also among the most prominent Medici art patrons, as he supported many major artists like Michelangelo and Botticelli.

Lorenzo de' Medici met Michelangelo while studying at the Academy of San Marco. Despite being a teen at the time, the artist impressed Lorenzo with his carving skills and got invited to stay at the place for two years. During his stay, Michelangelo became Donatello's student and formed lasting friendships with Lorenzo's sons, who would later become Popes Clement Vii and Leo X. The artist was later commissioned to paint the Sistine Chapel's upper walls by Pope Julius II and returned 25 years later to paint the Last Judgment. Donatello was also commissioned to create the world-renowned bronze David and the Judith and Holofernes.

Architectural Evolution

Tuscany's first Duke, Cosimo I de' Medici, initially established the Uffizi as an administrative center for the family. However, it was transformed into a public art gallery featuring numerous remarkable artworks, including Botticelli's "The Birth of Venus" and Bandinelli's "Laocoön and his Sons."

Cosimo the Elder commissioned the Duomo of Florence, which faced numerous delays due to the technical challenges architects faced while constructing it without Gothic buttresses. However, Brunelleschi proved that he could build the dome without the scaffolding, creating one of the world's tallest structures. Pope Leo X also oversaw the construction of St. Peter's Basilica, a project that Martin Luther questioned.

The Conspiracies and Resilience That Inspired Interesting Work

In 1478, Giuliano de' Medici and Lorenzo the Magnificent were attacked during a public mass. While the former died, Lorenzo the Magnificent survived with injuries. Witnessing the assassination attempt, angry citizens captured and killed the conspirators. The Medici family stayed in power, and the event was commemorated in art.

The Medici family was later exiled to Rome from 1494 to 1512 due to political issues and was replaced by an anti-Medici family. The statue of David, which was initially commissioned for religious purposes, was placed in the town hall. The government-oriented David's eye in Rome's direction, giving it a new political meaning.

During the Medici's exile, Machiavelli, a theorist and diplomat, networked with Anti-Medici figures. He was, therefore, placed on the Medici's list of conspirators as soon as they made it back to Florence. The philosopher was tortured and imprisoned but was eventually spared the execution on account of Pope Leo X. Machiavelli later dedicated "The Prince" to the next Medici ruler in hopes of securing a position within the court. Needless to say, his efforts failed.

Headway in the Worlds of Science, Music, and Fashion

The First Duke of Tuscany published a book about his telescope-based discoveries, which included his observation of Jupiter's moons, in 1610 after he was tutored by Galileo Galilei. The family also made musical advances, which included the financial support of significant opera houses. The piano was also invented by Bartolomeo Cristofori while he was working in the family's court.

Catherine de' Medici also made advancements in the worlds of fashion and equestrian sports. She commissioned a pair of high-heeled shoes because she wanted to appear taller, establishing the fashion statement as a symbol of wealth and status. This was a bold move on her part because, at the time, high heels were popular among butchers who wished to avoid getting blood on their feet. The noblewoman also popularized side-saddle riding so more women could ride without feeling exposed.

The Last of the Medici

The Medici bloodline ended with Gian Gastone de' Medici, Tuscany's last Grand Duke, who had no male heirs. Anne Maria Luisa de' Medici understood that Francis of Lorraine would inherit the power in Tuscany and that all her family's property would be automatically passed on to him. She, therefore, declared that everything that belonged to her family would remain in Florence to adorn the city, benefit its people, and attract foreigners.

28. The Borgia Family: A Papacy Marred by Scandal

The Borgia family is among the Renaissance's most famous yet controversial Italian noble families. The Borgias originally came from the Spanish Kingdom of Valencia and relocated to Italy. Their rule significantly influenced the history of Italy and the Catholic Church. Despite their scandalous stories and controversies, the family supported several artists and intellectuals at the time.

The Borgias' Ascent to Power

Alfonso de Borgia pursued a degree in canon and civil law, cultivating a successful career path in the field of politics as well as being invested in the church. He was a diocese representative and worked his way up until he became King Alfonso V of Aragon's secretary and Vice-Chancellor. He then became regent when the King went to conquer Naples.

Alfonso earned Rome's recognition and became both priest and bishop when he negotiated over a rival pope. A few years later, Alfonso traveled to Naples to reorganize the government before he represented Aragon at a council to reconcile the Western and Eastern churches. Although it failed, he established himself as a masterful diplomat.

Alfonso played a crucial role that helped the King negotiate papal approval for his rule of Naples and was therefore rewarded with the title cardinal in 1444. A year later, he moved to Rome at the age of 67. Unlike the rest of his family, he was an honest, sober, and dedicated man who would later create a more scandalous reputation for the family and Rome. One of Alfonso's nephews, Rodrigo, studied canon law and ended up working for the church. Although he had an esteemed job, he was infamous for his romantic pursuits. Alfonso's other nephew became a commander in the army.

Alfonso's Rise to Papacy

In the same year he returned to Rome, Alfonso was elected Pope because he wasn't involved with any major groups, and a short reigning period was ideal for his age. Upon receiving the title, Alfonso changed his name to Calixtus III. As a Spaniard ruling in Rome, Calixtus had several enemies. He followed a cautious ruling strategy to avoid them along with the major groups in the city. However, he didn't receive a warm welcome as the people rioted into his first ceremony. He also broke away from King Alfonso V after ignoring his request to go on a crusade.

Calixtus promoted his family, naming Rodrigo and his older brother, Pedro, cardinals and securing a range of positions for other family members. Being in their mid-20s, the brothers didn't take their positions seriously and engaged in acts that scandalized the city. Rodrigo was then made papal legate in another city, a position in which he demonstrated success and talent. He later became second in command of the church. Pedro also switched positions and was granted an army command. He, too, was very skillful and eventually became promoted to Prefect and Duke.

Pedro went on a mission to conquer Naples when King Alfonso V died. Many people believe that Calixtus planned to have Pedro rule over Naples. However, Pedro had to fight with rivals over the jurisdiction of Naples and soon died of malaria. Calixtus' death followed in 1458.

Rodrigo Finally Becomes Pope

Rodrigo played a role in electing Pius II as the next pope. He knew, however, that he was in danger because he was a young Spaniard without a patron. He then decided to establish himself as a salient ally to the Pope and secured his position as Vice-Chancellor. Rodrigo was capable of proving himself worthy of the title. However, what overpowered his skill was his love for money and women. He, therefore, didn't follow in his late uncle's footsteps and was even reprimanded by the Pope for his inappropriate conduct and romantic affairs. Instead of taking it as a serious warning and focusing more on his career, Rodrigo tried to become more discreet. Regardless of his cautiousness, Rodrigo ended up with many children. Cesare, born in 1475, and Lucrezia, who came to life five years later, were the most notable.

Pope Pius II died in 1464, and Rodrigo again influenced the decision of the election of the following pope: Pope Paul I. A few years later, Rodrigo was sent to Spain with the authority to either agree or disagree on the marriage of Ferdinand and Isabella. Approving their marriage would signal that he agrees with the union that would form between the Spanish regions Aragon and Castille; if he denies their marriage, he will deny the union between the regions.

Rodrigo accepted the marriage, earning King Ferdinand's support. He also used his position to name his son Duke and marry his daughters to build alliances. Instead of electing Rodrigo as pope, cardinals elected Innocent VIII. Rodrigo did everything he could to get to the throne. He even earned the support of Innocent, who resulted in a lot of chaos before he died. Rodrigo continued bribing people in positions of power until he finally bought himself the papacy. He was then renamed Pope Alexander VI.

Pope Alexander VI

Surprisingly, Pope Alexander VI gained the support of the public. Although he was a skilled diplomat, he led an ostentatious, hedonistic lifestyle. Alexander couldn't separate his position and wealth from his family, so his son was soon named cardinal. The rest of his family arrived and settled all over Italy to reap their share of the rewards. Although nepotism was common in the papacy, Alexander went very far in abusing his position.

He had various mistresses and affairs, which tainted the church's image. Further disorder ensued when his children started getting in trouble with the families they married into. Alexander tried to salvage the situation through negations, which involved marrying off Lucrezia, who was 12 at the time, to Giovanni Sforza. He later divorced the couple when Giovanni opposed him.

Alexander retired to a palace instead of choosing to flee when King Charles VIII of France invaded Italy. He believed he could negotiate a compromise that guaranteed his life along with an independent papacy. France seized control of Naples, and Alexander played a role in getting the rest of Italy to unite. However, he knew it was time to flee when King Charles returned to Rome.

Cesare Borgia

In 1498, Pope Alexander formed an alliance with the new French King, Louis XIII, granting Cesare the title Duke of Valence. Cesare also married into the King's family and earned an army. The Duke went back to Italy, embarking on a remarkable career path in the military, and never saw his pregnant wife and his soon-to-be child again.

Cesare's military success brought him power over his father.
https://commons.wikimedia.org/wiki/File:Cesareborgia.jpg

Cesare's military success brought him power over his father, and those who wanted to set appointments with the papacy found it more economical to speak to him rather than Alexander. Cesare earned the title of Captain-General of the army of the church. However, many people attributed the death of Lucrezia's husband, along with other unsolved murders, to him. Cesare's conquests left the family under control of a large amount of land. Lucrezia was also sent to marry Alfonso d'Este to secure Cesare's strategy.

The Fall of the Borgias

Cesare soon recognized that his alliance with France was no longer beneficial. After he planned everything needed to break away, his father died of malaria in 1503. Alexander was his benefactor; his lands weren't united yet, and he was also very ill. Cesare was forced to flee after his enemies came back from exile to fight. The new pope arrested Cesare. He also threw out most of the Borgias from their positions and controlled the others. After Cesare was released, he went to Naples, where Ferdinand of Aragon arrested him again. He managed to escape two years later but ended up murdered in 1507 when he was only 31 at the time.

Lucrezia Borgia

Lucrezia made amends with her husband and his family. She also reconciled with her state, where she became regent and took up positions in court. She patronized several artists, creating a court with substantial beauty and culture. She oversaw the state even through war. She was loved among the people and died in 1519 when she was 39.

29. The Sforza of Milan: Warriors and Patrons

The Sforza family was first known by the name Attendoli. This humble Italian family produced who would later be among the two most popular fortunes, giving rise to a dynasty whose rulership lasted for nearly a century. The Attendoli were a wealthy family of farmers who only assumed the name Sforza, which translates to force, when Muzio Attendolo, the dynasty's founder, came by. Muzio and his son Francesco were both mercenary army commanders. Francesco was named Duke of Milan when he married Duke Filippo Maria Visconti's daughter, Bianca, in 1450.

Francesco Sforza: The Patron of Art and Architecture

Francesco and Biancagave gave birth to Galeazzo Maria Sforza in 1444. Three years later, Duke Filippo Visconti died without a legitimate male heir. The Milanese thought it was an opportunity to establish the Ambrosian Republic, which later fell due to a financial crisis. They hired Francesco to maintain order in Milan. However, he decided to take advantage of the situation and form an allegiance with Venice. He borrowed money from the Medici family to establish strong troops and besieged Milan until the new government surrendered in 1450.

He hired Filatrete, who wrote a treatise representing himself as an architect, and Francesco, the patron, conversed about an ideal city called Sforzinda. Francesco ordered the continuity of projects that the Visconti had already started and commissioned the creation of new ones. He continued supporting the construction of the Milan Cathedral and the Certosa di Pavia. He also commissioned the Ospedale Maggiore and a church in the monastery of the Santa Maria delle Grazie.

Galeazzo Maria Sforza

Galeazzo Maria Sforza proved to be a capable ruler after his father died in 1466. Although he was considered ostentatious, authoritarian, and extravagant, Galeazzo Maria was great at his job. He was responsible for many projects that supported the field of agriculture, such as the construction of irrigation and transportation canals and the introduction of rice cultivation. He also played a role in boosting commerce and encouraging the manufacture of textiles like wool and silk. Galeazzo also contributed to the enrichment of Milan's culture by patronizing several poets, musicians, scholars, and artists. Some inadequacies in his political strategy led to Milan's isolation. He also ended up murdered by three conspirators on Christmas.

Ludovico Sforza

Ludovico Sforza, Galeazzo's brother, played a great role in the advancement of arts and politics during the Renaissance. He married Beatrice d'Este, who died while giving birth to their two sons in 1497. Ludovico tried to establish an allegiance with France to destabilize his enemies by encouraging King Charles VIII to invade the rest of Italy. However, diplomacy wasn't his strongest suit, and his pact resulted in the French occupation of Milan in 1499. He eventually died while he was imprisoned by the French in 1508.

Despite his political downfall, Ludovico was a significant patron of the arts. He commissioned several major artists like Bramante and Leonardo da Vinci, who worked on several prominent projects like The Last Supper. He also commissioned numerous architectural projects, including renovating several Milanese churches and constructing the Piazza Ducale in Vigevano.

The Medici, Borgia, and Sforza are among the most significant families of the Italian Renaissance. Their power and contributions left a lasting influence on the region. The Medicis were generous patrons of the arts and pioneers of transformative financial concepts who transformed Florence into a cultural center. Although the Borgias were controversial, they played a key role in supporting several artists and scholars, and the Sforzas shaped Milan's political, architectural, and artistic landscape.

Chapter 7: Exploration and Expansion Stories

Expansion and exploration made the world feel a lot smaller and more accessible. Formations of new countries like the United States are because the age of exploration allowed for new cultures to uniquely form in different parts of the world. Furthermore, expansion, along with the development of new technology, is what created the globalized world that people live in today. As much as the adventuring spirit of those who discovered new parts of the world can be admired, the atrocities that were committed in the name of empires and religion cannot be overlooked.

Therefore, it is essential to honestly explore how the European world interacted with the indigenous people they encountered and how the wealth of the Western world grew due to exploration. The complex relationship between discovery and ethnic and religious identities can be told through the stories of the explorers who stepped out of Europe into the unknown. Looking into the details of expansion stories in the imperialist age can reveal how the world was divided and how it influenced modern culture. Colonization and conquering are central parts of European history that perfectly contrast the highest and lowest points of the human drive to explore.

30. Columbus and the Discovery of the New World

It is somewhat of a misnomer to claim that Christopher Columbus discovered the Americas; however, that does not detract from the incredible feat of expansion journeying into these unknown territories. Columbus was the first European to set foot in America. The continent's discovery helped Spain exponentially grow its wealth in the era. Furthermore, it was the beginning of the American project, which the world has seen grow into the international superpower it is today.

Christopher Columbus discovered the Americas.

The sail routes to Asia, where valuable resources like spices could be traded, were controlled by the Ottoman Empire at the time. The Columbus voyage aimed to find a route to Asia by sailing west from Europe. Columbus was an Italian native, but his journey was sponsored by Spanish Catholic Monarchs who were inspired because they had defeated the Moors in Grenada. The renewed national spirit gave the Spanish Empire adventurous aspirations. On August 3rd, 1492, Columbus left the coast of Spain on three ships: the Santa Maria, the Pinta, and the Nina.

By October 12th, Columbus first encountered land in the Bahamas, which he believed to be the Indies. He named the island San Salvador and claimed it for Spain. Columbus's voyage continued as he reached Cuba, thinking it was mainland China. He traveled to Haiti and the Dominican Republic, mistakenly assuming the islands were Japan. He named the islands Hispaniola, where Columbus established a small colony of 39 men. In March 1493, the explorer finally returned to Spain with captives from the newfound lands as well as gold and spices. Columbus received the highest praise upon his return.

Columbus journeyed back to the New World another three times in 1493, 1498, and 1502, before he died in 1506. The gold that Columbus acquired made him a wealthy man, and the blueprint that he had set out helped transform Spain into one of the wealthiest nations in the century that followed. It can be argued that Europe would not have been able to establish itself as a global force without Columbus' brave venture into the New World. Columbus was one of the key figures in the Age of Exploration and is seen as an inspiration to many for venturing bravely into the unknown. His influence in the region he discovered can still be felt today, with Islands like Haiti and much of South America still being largely Catholic.

Although many honor Columbus as a great explorer and pioneer of European excellence, his accomplishments are not without controversy. Many today highlight that his treatment of Natives was atrocious and unacceptable. Since the Native people of the islands did not practice Catholicism, Columbus saw them as pagans who were worthy of ill-treatment in the name of the Lord. He saw himself as their superior who needed to religiously educate them. October 9th is celebrated as Columbus Day, but due to the controversies attached to his expansion of the Spanish Empire, some choose to celebrate it as Indigenous Day instead so that the native people could be honored as well.

31. Vasco Da Gama: Finding the Sea Route to India

Vasco Da Gama was the first European to find an ocean route from Europe to India.

Vasco Da Gama was the first European to find an ocean route from Europe to India. Da Gama's journey followed Bartholomew Dias, who had sailed along the coast of West Africa to what is now known as South Africa from Portugal. Dias applied to complete the journey rounding the Southern tip of Africa to India, but the Crown put Da Gama in charge of the voyage. The journey's goal was to avoid the land-bound trade routes that had historically been used for commerce between Africa, the Middle East, and the Italians. Furthermore, the Da Gama and the Portuguese crown believed they could ally with Christian nations against the Middle East and North African Islamic empires.

Da Gama's expedition commenced in 1497. He arrived on the Southwest coast of India in 1498. Two new ships were built for Da Gama's treacherous journey, with an additional two being added. Da Gama captained the Sao Gabriel, and his brother Paulo Coelho was in charge of the Sao Rapahel. The biggest of the four ships was captained by another one of Da Gama's brothers, Nicolau Coelho. The third ship was called the Berrio and was able to carry 200 tons of merchandise. The large size of the Berrio can draw a picture of how large the operation was intended to be to exploit this newly carved-out trade route.

Dias's strategy differed from Da Gama's insofar as he stayed close to the coastline, battling the rough waters and raging winds, while Da Gama strayed off further into the ocean, where he made use of winds that favored their journey. When Da Gama reached Southern Africa on November 22nd in the area now known as Mossel Bay, the crew decided that they would dismantle the biggest ship and split the supplies and crew between the three ships that remained.

Sailing in those days was no easy feat. The crew subsisted on hardened biscuits that they would bang against the hard wooden floors of the ships to get the bugs out. These almost inedible biscuits were supplemented with a dash of olive oil and a splash of water. They would then have salted beef or pork on some days; on other days, it was rice or cheese on the menu. Only the highest-ranking members of the crew were allowed to enjoy some dried fruit. The nutrient-scarce diet resulted in many crew members developing scurvy, a disease caused by a lack of vitamin C. When they reached the East Coast of Africa in Mobassa on April 7th, they were assisted by locals who knew how to cure the disease. The crew members suffering from scurvy were given oranges before fully recovering to continue the mission.

Da Gama arrived in India on May 18th, 1498. Their ships were fully loaded with rare spices like pepper and cinnamon before they made their journey back to Europe. Many more crew members died from scurvy on the way back because they were unable to get treated this time around. The second voyage Da Gam made in 1502 was less diplomatic as the explorer came with blood on his mind. The region was conquered, and Da Gama was crowned as the Viceroy of Portugal in the area. The work of Vaco Da Gama and Christopher Columbus propelled Europe into the age of imperialism, as many nations from the continent began conquering the world.

32. The Treaty of Tordesillas: Dividing the World

The Treaty of Tordesillas was signed to divide the Americas between two of the biggest superpowers at the time, Spain and Portugal. The discoveries of Columbus meant that there were new opportunities for empires to expand to grow their influence and wealth. Since these new territories were unclaimed in the European world, it opened the door for conflicts and disagreements. The Catholic Church had a lot of power at the time, so the Spanish rulers Queen Isabella I and King Ferdinand II sought help from Pope Alexander VI to make claims on these new lands without interference from Portugal or any other powerful Christian kingdoms.

The Pope issued a Papal bull that drew a dividing line that spanned about 320 miles west of the Cape Verde Islands. Spain was permitted to claim any lands west of the line, while Portugal was able to conquer lands east of the demarcation. Furthermore, the Pope declared that any lands owned by the Church were not to be touched. King John II was dissatisfied with the agreement because he believed that the bull tied his kingdom's hands in terms of claiming newly discovered land in the new world that Columbus had revealed. Moreover, the King claimed that there was not enough space at sea to freely move between the African continent and Europe.

To address the concerns of the Portuguese Empire, a meeting was set up in Tordesillas, Spain. Ambassadors from Spain and Portugal agreed to shift the dividing line to 1185 miles west of Cape Verde. In 1506, Pope Julius II sanctioned the change of the positioning of the line. This shift allowed Portugal to conquer Brazil, which was later discovered by Pedro Alvarez Cabral (This is why modern Brazilians are Portuguese speakers; the Portuguese territory was expanded inland into South America.)

Since the native populations of the Americas were not Christian, they were allowed to be conquered. The stipulation that Pope Alexander VI added meant that Spain and Portugal were not allowed to overthrow any Christian kings. The treaty was between Spain and Portugal, so the agreement did not consider other European empires like the British and Dutch. However, other European superpowers only claimed lands in the new world much later on. Considering that indigenous cultures like the

Aztecs, Inca, and Tainos did not have a Christian king, they violently suffered during this colonial period.

33. Conquistadors and the Fall of Empires: The Aztecs and Incas

The Incan Empire was formed by conquering neighboring tribes in Peru. In 1533, the empire spanned vast lands and was the largest in the world. Like their European counterparts, the Inca used religion to conquer because their cosmology asserted that they had a divine right to rule. The Inca believed they were chosen people descended from their Sun deity, Inti. The Incas were on the brink of collapse when the explorer and conquistador Francisco Pizarro entered the picture. The conquered tribes under the Incan Empire could not integrate, which caused civil unrest, and European diseases that the Incas had no immunity to were ravaging the population.

Pizarro and his Spanish forces were able to defeat the Inca easily due to the superior European weapons, as well as the local inclination to rebel against their Incan oppressors. The collaboration with local warriors resulted in the Europeans being able to overthrow the powerful Incan Empire in one generation. The Inca had vast riches and dwelled in resource-filled Peru. Therefore, the conquistadors had ample motivation to conquer the region.

Francisco Pizarro and his partner Diego de Almagro had not achieved the renown that they yearned for in their own country as adventurers and treasure hunters. The discovery of South American riches was an opportunity for the two to make a name for themselves. They had seen how other conquistadors made fortunes in Mexico, so they aimed to emulate and recreate that success. The political instability among the Inca resulted in Spain being able to conquer the area by 1514; however, the transition was not smooth because the Spanish also experienced internal fighting that caused the murder of Pizarro.

Similar to the Inca, the Aztecs were also a conquering nation. The nation controlled about 500 different states who were required to pay tributes to their Aztec rulers. Furthermore, the Aztecs practiced human sacrifice, which bred resentment among some of the groups under the empire. Hernan Cortes was able to practice diplomacy to get the support of rebel forces under various chiefs. They captured the Aztec capital of Tenochtitlan with the help of local fighters. Smallpox also played a big role in devastating much of the indigenous population.

The historical drama did not end when Cortes took over the capital. A group of Spaniards were sent over to Mexico with orders to arrest Cortes when they arrived. Cortes defeated the arresting party with a surprise attack and convinced many of the soldiers to help him with his ambitions to conquer the Aztec Empire. However, Officer Pedro de Alvarado, whom Cortes had left in charge, had massacred many of the Aztec people while the leaders were gone. De Alvarado's actions caused the locals to rebel. Emperor Montezuma, who was Cortes's Aztec ally, was commanded to put an end to the rebellion immediately, but he had lost favor with his people and was unable to influence them effectively. The Emperor died trying to stop the unrest. Eventually, the Aztec Empire completely collapsed under Spanish rule because of the superior European weaponry and the death caused by foreign diseases. This is why modern Mexicans speak Spanish.

34. The Slave Trade: A Dark Chapter in Exploration

The transatlantic slave trade is one of the darkest stains on the development of the Western world. The dehumanizing atrocities committed during the slave trade are almost unimaginable in the modern world, where people are protected by human rights considerations. Slavery was a common practice when the transatlantic slave trade began bringing people of African descent to the Caribbean, as well as the Americas. The trade of humans spanned from the sixteenth to the nineteenth century. Much of the economies of European nations were propped up with the trade of enslaved people, so African people were an integral part of the European story at its foundation.

Many people have an unrealistic image of how the slave trade took place. Europeans did not run into Africa, rounding up people to sell. Slave traders bartered with Africans who captured enslaved people and would trade with them for metals, ammunition, beads, and other goods. In 1444, Portuguese marauders aimed to go into Senegal with their superior weapons to capture enslaved people in the country. However, the Senegalese people were avid sailors and were able to outmaneuver the Europeans in the shallow waters off the coast. Therefore, the Portuguese slave traders were forced to trade with the African locals as opposed to using military action. As the European demand for enslaved people increased, they began fuelling wars between rival groups in Africa, facilitating the capturing of more people to sell. It is estimated that the entire slave trade captured over 15 million Africans. Furthermore, multiple generations were born into captivity and traded as commodities.

The slave trade was justified by religion, as many pastors preached sermons about how men have dominion over beasts. In this perception of the world, enslaved Africans were seen as animals that could be likened to livestock. This dehumanization of enslaved Africans resulted in terrible treatment as they were beaten, tortured, and sometimes fought for the entertainment of their European masters. The negative impacts of the slave trade are still being experienced today, as many people in the African diaspora have lower socioeconomic positions in society globally. This social impact is a result of generational oppression derailing the development of African people abroad while colonization destabilized people on the continent.

Exploration, expansion, and colonization are complex topics to fully unpack. Much of what is enjoyed in the developed world is a result of this conquest. Without this chapter in history, Europe and the United States as we know it today may have never existed. However, some of the problems that the developing world is still dealing with today are a direct result of slavery and colonization. Therefore, a knife's edge has to be walked between the adventuring heroes that are honored and celebrated and the condemnation of some of their darker actions.

A mistake many people make is weighing past actions against the moral or ethical standards that we have now. The age of conquest was a different period when people had a completely foreign way of understanding the world compared to modern sensibilities. Therefore, as much as condemnation is due for the murderous, genocidal, and oppressive actions of European travelers, conquerors, and settlers, it is also important to note that it was a step toward developing the more humane perceptions people have now.

The bravery it took to venture out into an unknown world on treacherous seas, experiencing untold discomfort, is admirable. The people who had the guts to go out on these journeys of discovery must not be forgotten, but in the same breath, the cultures that suffered under European oppression must also be uplifted as central to the European story. The tales of Europe expanding into the globe are a balance of the adventuring spirit building new ways of life worldwide while oppressing people who were different from them.

Chapter 8: Enlightenment, Retribution, and Revolution Stories

From the late 17th to the early 19th century, a series of uprisings and revolutions marked Europe's history. This chapter aims to capture the transformative period known as the Enlightenment and how its ideas fueled social and political revolts. Also known as the "Age of Reason," the period of Enlightenment brought on new philosophies that challenged traditional authority and embraced reason, liberty, and progress, shaping philosophical, political, and scientific discourse.

Renowned thinkers of this era created a massive change in reforming thinking and reason, laying the foundation for modern thought. Imagine centuries of traditional beliefs being set aside in just a few decades. This is what the Enlightenment was like. Instead of age-old customs, it gave way to individualism, exploration, scientific discoveries, tolerance, and political and industrial revolutions.

Thinkers of the Enlightenment were inspired by ancient Roman and Greek civilizations.

The origins of this period can be traced back to the aftermath of the English Civil Wars. During this time, the power of the ever-present autocratic monarchy was restored, beginning with giving back the reign to Charles II in 1660. This fueled dissatisfaction among the political thinkers at the time, who now began to consider the many ways the country would benefit from different political and societal structures. Their ideas launched movements demanding political change, which eventually occurred in 1688/89 when William and Mary were given the throne (known as the Glorious Revolution).

Thinkers of the Enlightenment were inspired by ancient Roman and Greek civilizations, citing how modern society would benefit from modeling these. It was an undeniably different idea from the centuries of political tyranny and dissolution of personal rights and well-being people experienced across Europe. John Locke, an English physician and philosopher, saw the answer in the separation of the government and the church. He believed this would encourage religious toleration, fighting for people's rights and property ownership (proposing an early form of social contract between people and the state).

Locke also claimed that human consciousness was the gateway to true liberty, and he dismissed the ancient (but highly prevailing at the time) notion that knowledge is an elusive and secretive entity and could only be obtained through mystical ways. Locke's ideas reflected the beliefs of

Thomas Hobbes, who also advocated for social contracts between the people and the government, seeing it as the key to people's contentment. Grand promises notwithstanding, these ideas and the revolution they caused often faced retribution from the old regimes.

35. Voltaire: Champion of Enlightenment and Free Thought

Voltaire (born François-Marie Arouet) was a pivotal figure in the Enlightenment. He was a prolific French writer, philosopher, and historian. Through his versatile career, he advocated for freedom of speech and faith. He also supported the notion of creating a divide between the government and the church. In the age of aristocratic tyranny, this wasn't a small feat. Voltaire had to fight against the French censorship laws that prohibited the publication of anything that went against the ideas of the Church or the main French political institutions.

Fortunately, Voltaire was very clever, as illustrated by the following story. Once, he returned an insult to a nobleman and was arrested despite not being the one initiating the conflict. He managed to negotiate his release from the Bastille and got himself exiled to England instead. Witnessing the benefits of Britain's constitutional monarchy, Voltaire became even more passionate about freedom of speech and personal liberty.

From England, Voltaire continued to critique the French state and the Church's power over it. He wrote several novels ridiculing the government, religion, theologians, and everything and everyone oppressing the commoners. In them, Voltaire argued the unfairness of the fact that the latter had to shoulder the burden of taxation while nobility, officials, and church officials were exempt. One of his recurring themes was a hero going through unimaginable hurdles only to have them reassured by noblemen that it was for their benefit.

Some credit his prolific creativity to his excessive caffeine consumption (he reportedly could drink up to 70 cups of coffee a day!) Whatever was behind his thoughts and beliefs, Voltaire became a true champion of freedom in Britain and America. His principles become widely recognized and accepted across other developed countries as well. However, not all countries were on board with allowing freedom of religious expression. Some would imprison and execute those who publicly spoke about these new, revolutionary, enlightened ideas - as well as those accused of doing so. Voltaire knew that in some countries, states, and religions, united would always oppress the freedom of independent thinking. However, until his death, he continued to encourage people to oppose these violent and oppressive regimes, not allowing them to silence anyone who disagreed with their way of thinking.

36. The Social Contract: Rousseau's Revolutionary Idea

After Locke and others popularized the idea of social contracts, the concurrent requests for political change in France at the dawn of the 18th century pushed the notion forward. Diderot, for example, claimed that by expanding reason (provided by a contract in which the state allows people to develop independent and critical thinking), people would be able to keep destructive passions in check and maintain their virtue.

A similar idea was proclaimed by Jean-Jacques Rousseau, who argued that people were rational by birth. However, when they lost their freedom due to societal constraints, their reason was suppressed, and they became unable to think rationally. Moreover, civilized society made people unhappy, and to change this, people should seek closeness with nature, away from the oppressive society.

Rousseau also claimed that true political sovereignty was possible – but could only be obtained by people when the laws were adequately maintained and the rulings respected. This thought was expressed in one of Rousseu's most renowned works, The Social Contract, in which he argued that people could only be free if their society granted them certain rights and ensured their well-being. This required a democratic government, which was a radical political notion at the time. However, in just a few decades, the same idea influenced some of the most significant revolutionary movements, including the famous French Revolution. Even revolutionaries like Robespierre were inspired by Rousseu's works and philosophy.

For the same reason, they were blamed by the French government for terrible acts they never committed. Despite this, The Social Contract became one of European political history's most influential pieces of literature. To this day, the ideas it dissects continue to inspire by emphasizing the importance of being a responsible part of society to ensure liberty and well-being.

37. The Storming of the Bastille: Spark of the French Revolution

By the summer of 1789, France was well on its way to a full-blown revolution. The governor of the Bastille - the fortress that served as the most infamous prison at the time - knew that the revolutionaries could target the building and asked for help. He had reasons to fear defeat. The guardians of the fortress were mere veterans no longer capable of serving in the battle. A few more capable soldiers arrived, but there were also uncontrollable protests in the city several days beforehand. After that, the Bastille received reinforcements of 250 barrels of gunpowder, distributed among the guards as they raised the drawbridges. Unfortunately, this was proven to be a little too late. When they heard that King Luis was planning to arrest the brand new National Assembly that promised more power to people, the Parisians got infuriated. On July 14, 1789, they armed themselves with swords, muskets, and other makeshift weapons and began to gather around the fortress.

Reports account for nine hundred Parisians gathering outside the fortress that morning, led by three delegates from the Hôtel de Ville (the seat of city government), who presented the rebel's demands. Not wanting to do the dishonorable act of capitulating before the enemy without authorization from the King, the governor refused to surrender at first. However, he withdrew the cannons from the walls to show he had no intention of inflicting harm on anyone. One of the delegates saw this with their own eyes and went to announce it to the mob, but it was too late. By the time they returned down to the base of the fortress, two agile revolutionaries had climbed the walls and cut the chain of the drawbridge, causing it to fall. From then on, there was no way to de-escalate the situation. People would become trapped and die under the bridge, while others started to run across into the yard. They were under the misconception that the guards let them in. However, the guards knew nothing about this, and when they saw the crowd surging in, they began to shoot in panic. In turn, the people thought that they'd been lured into a trap, and those with weapons proceeded to attack.

While the revolutionaries were fighting the guards of the Bastille, the French Guards' rebellious members and other defecting soldiers heard of what was happening and joined the battle. Their organization was a little haphazard, but they brought valuable reinforcement to the crowd, including cannons they fired at the Bastille's gate. While the governor still considered a counterattack at this time, his men talked him out of it. Seeing no other option but to surrender, the governor raised the white flag and let the other drawbridge down. After all, he had no backup. The royal army fled the city by this time, trying to get as far ahead as possible to avoid the mob reaching them, eventually settling in Versailles, where the King resided.

After flooding the Bastille, the revolutionaries liberated the prisoners, disarmed the remaining guards (several of them died or were lynched during or immediately after the attack), and seized the ammunition. The governor's leading officers were killed, and he was taken to the Hôtel de Ville, where his future punishment was to be determined. However, not wanting anyone else to decide his fate, the governor provoked one of his captors to attack and kill him.

When the news of the Bastille's siege reached King Louis XVI in Versailles, he made a last attempt to stop the revolution. He returned to function the Jacques Necker, the chief minister whom he removed for not preventing the rise of the National Assembly. However, the reversal of this decision didn't satisfy the crowd anymore. With the fall of the Bastille, the revolution officially started, and there was no stopping it now. Four years later, shortly after the French monarchy was abolished, King Louis and his wife Marie Antoinette were captured and executed for treason.

As the revolution began, there were talks about turning the Bastille into a museum or even a base for volunteers. However, with the building's past and sheer size, the Permanent Committee of Municipal Electors couldn't justify its upkeep anymore (it was hardly worth it before, given the small number of prisoners it housed) and authorized its demolition. A park was built in its place, standing as a homage to Parisians' first victory during the revolution. However, the people weren't left without tangible memories of this event (despite sacking the idea of the museum). Wanting to promote the victory and its significance, one of the people doing the demolition seized some of the Bastille remains and converted them into souvenirs. The different items seized were sold quickly. Fans from its papers were the ladies' favorites, while gentlemen preferred paperweights from the rocks once held up the fortress. There were even miniature replicas of the building to buy. People from other parts of France came to Paris to get a good deal on the Bastille stones. They took these home, inspired to contribute to the revolution themselves.

Today, the fortress's outline and a small portion of the foundation remain a symbol of how people joining forces brought an end to a failing regime and gave momentum to the French revolutionary rationale.

38. The Declaration of Rights of Man and Citizen: A Revolutionary Document

No narrative of the Enlightenment would be complete without mentioning the Declaration of the Rights of Man and the Citizen. Issued on 26th August 1789 by the French National Constituent Assembly, under the original name of *Déclaration des droits de l'homme et du citoyen*, this was the first document clearly outlining the individual and collective rights of people during the French Revolution. The document's creators took inspiration from constitutional pieces like the Magna Carta and the revolutionary ideas spreading across the United States, which led to the signing of the Declaration of Independence. There were unmistakable differences. For example, The Declaration of the Rights of Man and the Citizen emphasizes that people's rights are universal and inviolable and should come naturally to be upheld.

However, the influence of the Magna Carta was undeniable. Declaration of the Rights of Man and the Citizen also talks about making monarch subordinates to the law, proclaims that no one should be arrested, imprisoned, or accused without lawfully established causes, and mandates that taxation will require common consent. The authors also worked with Thomas Jefferson in the past, who inspired the Magna Carta and left his mark on the Declaration of the Rights of Man and the Citizen. This was seen in the clause talking about the innate freedom of people and the need for them to remain this way, thus having equal rights.

39. Immanuel Kant: Reason and Enlightenment

Influenced by Rousseau and Descartes, German philosopher Immanuel Kant was another remarkable character during the Enlightenment. Born and raised in Koenigsberg (modern-day Russia) in 1781, Kant began publishing works that laid the foundations for modern philosophy. As his publications began to mount, he likened his efforts to enlighten people to that of Copernicus, and rightfully so. He inspired many other philosophers – whose work was simply called post-Kantian.

IMMANUEL KANT
From a painting

Kant was influenced by Rousseau and Descartes.
https://commons.wikimedia.org/wiki/File:Immanuel_Kant_3.jpg

However, Kant's road to success in modernizing philosophy wasn't exactly smooth. When he began to explore the scene, there were two major camps of European thinkers. The empiricists, like Hume, Locke, Bacon, and Berkeley, prevailed in Britain. Whereas the rationalists ruled the rest of the continent. Their ranks included Spinoza, Leibniz, and Descartes. They claimed that a belief must be certified through reasoning to be seen as knowledge. This included inferential steps from unshakable principles –either self-evident to whoever observed them or couldn't be denied. According to the rationalist, these axioms already exist in everyone. In other words, every person was born with the innate ability to recognize them. By contrast, empiricists considered this idea an illusion. They argued that knowledge can only be obtained through hard work and experience – when people use their senses to consolidate new information into their minds. However, this information is bound to be inaccurate and subject to change due to future learning experiences.

In a never-before-seen move, Kant found a way to consolidate rationalist and empirical ideas into one solid thought form. Many describe his way of incorporating their strongest aspects while displaying their inadequacies radically revamping. At first, he was heavily criticized for turning the centuries-old traditional beliefs on their head. However, as other great thinkers dived deeper into his reasoning, more and more people ruled out the conventional concerns. Soon, they didn't even find them worth pursuing during philosophical debates discussing the nature of knowledge.

The reasoning behind Kant's reformative ideas and methods was also shocking at the time – given it was connected to metaphysical principles (Kant bound philosophy to science). The followers of the ancient traditions his ideas pushed aside and modernist thinkers at the time both disregarded the notion that people's knowledge could be tied to external objects. While some played with the concept of "objects of knowledge," most found their existence unimaginable. It was common sense to think that the subject of knowledge would exist separately from physical objects – except Kant disagreed. Inspired by Copernicus's idea that the earth circles around the sun and not the other way around (as it was believed at the time), Kant proposed to change the assumption that people's knowledge can transcend the nature of objects and consider that the objects can conform to peoples way of acquiring knowledge. This required inverted thinking – just as astronomers had to invert their theory of the sun and earth to resolve the difficulties they encountered during their research. In other words, by changing perspectives, the notion of the objects of knowledge wouldn't seem unimaginable anymore.

The above recounting of Kant's work is only a snippet of its effort toward expanding the philosophies revolving around reason. Another example can be found in his publication titled "What is Enlightenment?" in which he attempted to answer age-old questions troubling thinkers. They lived in it for a while now, yet they couldn't define it. According to

Kant, the Enlightenment is nothing but one's way of breaking free of a state of unknowing and being led by others and their knowledge. It's like a child starting to use his reason and understanding to learn what he needs to survive and thrive as he grows into adulthood. It's not letting someone else tell you how and what to think. It's having the courage to break free from others' tutelage and use the reason you were born with. Don't think you can't do it and make up your mind. Don't be afraid to come to your own resolutions.

Kant argued that following one's own reason leads to a faculty shared by all able-minded people on earth. If one also accepts his notion that reason is an innate capacity rather than a learned skill, the conclusion is simple. Everyone can learn the same things in the same way.

By putting this idea in the essay "*What Is Enlightenment?*" in front of the general public, Kant took a massive risk. He had his reputation as a renowned philosopher at stake, and this wasn't a notion everyone was prepared to embrace. Fortunately, with this work – along with his other publication, *"Critique of Pure Reason"*- he was able to not only uphold but further grow the number of his supporters across Europe. While these works were published in Berlin, his assumptions were shared by many and were seen on the other side of the continent as well – including some of the central characters of the French Revolution that was soon to follow.

Chapter 9: Napoleon Bonaparte: Stories of His Rise and Fall

Napoleon Bonaparte, the diminutive dynamo of the 19th century, was a man whose stature may have been short but whose ambitions reached towering heights. With a penchant for conquering both territory and hearts, this Corsican-born general-turned-emperor reshaped the map of Europe and redefined the art of warfare. You can't learn about Europe's history without coming across this influential figure. His cunning strategies were as sharp as his iconic bicorne hat, and his charisma, like a fine French wine, left a lasting impression on history. Whether you view him as a military genius or a power-hungry conqueror, one thing is certain: Napoleon was a figure who refused to be confined by the limits of his stature, leaving an indelible mark on the world stage. You can admire his audacity or question his audaciousness, but there's no denying that Napoleon Bonaparte was a man who knew how to make history dance to his imperial tune.

Napoleon refused to be confined by the limits of his stature.

40. Napoleon: From Corsica to Emperor

In his early years, Napoleon Bonaparte, known as Napoleone di Buonaparte, came into the world on August 15th, 1769, in the picturesque town of Ajaccio on the island of Corsica. Napoleon's family occupied a unique social niche between the haute bourgeoisie and minor nobility. His ancestry was a subject of speculation, with Napoleon dismissing extravagant claims and asserting his Corsican roots. Napoleon's Corsican heritage with Italian roots became a target for detractors who sought to tarnish his image. Early British biographer William Burdon attributed his character's supposed "dark ferocity" to his Italian ancestry, unfairly likening him to Italian treachery rather than embracing French openness and vivacity. The British journalist William Cobbett even dismissed him as a "low-bred upstart from the contemptible island of Corsica." Yet, despite these prejudices, Napoleon's actions defied stereotypes.

At nine, Napoleon's father secured their family's recognition as Corsican nobility, enabling him to apply for royal bursaries for his sons' education. Napoleon's journey to becoming a French officer and gentleman was set in motion when he received one of these bursaries, allowing him to embark on his education in France. Napoleon excelled in mathematics, a subject he later found crucial for military leadership. Napoleon's exceptional intellect and aptitude for mathematics led him to choose a career in the prestigious artillery rather than the navy. He excelled academically, impressing his teachers and receiving recommendations for further education in prestigious institutions. His decision to join the artillery marked him as part of an elite group, and he became the first Corsican to attend the École Royale Militaire in Paris.

Napoleon completed his studies at Brienne and entered the École Royale Militaire in Paris in 1784. On September 1st, 1785, Napoleon received his commission into the Compagnie d'Autume of bombardiers within the 5th Brigade of the 1st Battalion of the Régiment de la Fère, stationed at Valence on the left bank of the Rhône. At just sixteen, he was among the youngest officers and the only Corsican holding an artillery commission in the French army. By late May 1788, Napoleon was stationed at the School of Artillery in Auxonne, eastern France, not far from Dijon.

In April 1789, he was sent to Seurre to help put down a riot, showing his willingness to maintain order and discipline. This is when his career truly began. However, the political situation in France was rapidly evolving, leading to the outbreak of the French Revolution on July 14, 1789, with the storming of the Bastille. Napoleon's reign was defined by his military conquests. One of Napoleon's most celebrated achievements was his series of Italian campaigns in the late 1790s. His military brilliance was on full display as he defeated a series of Austrian and Italian armies, expanding French territory and establishing new republics in the process. These campaigns showcased his tactical genius and his ability to inspire his troops. The famous "Whiff of Grapeshot" in 1795, where he quelled a Parisian mob, further solidified his reputation as a military savior.

In 1799, the political landscape of France shifted dramatically. The Directory, the existing government, was beset by corruption and instability. In a coup d'état known as the 18 Brumaire, Napoleon overthrew the Directory and established the Consulate, with himself as First Consul. This marked the beginning of his effective rule over

France. In 1804, he declared himself Emperor of the French, effectively ending the French Revolution's egalitarian ideals. His coronation at Notre Dame Cathedral in Paris was a grand spectacle, showcasing his power and influence. As Emperor, he implemented numerous reforms that modernized France, including the Napoleonic Code, which laid the foundation for many modern legal systems.

41. The Napoleonic Code: A Legal Legacy

Napoleon's ascent to power in France in the late 18th century coincided with the tumultuous era of the French Revolution. With the old legal system in disarray, legal reform was urgently needed. Napoleon recognized this opportunity to consolidate his power and establish a legal code that would underpin his rule. He appointed a commission of jurists, headed by Jean-Jacques Régis de Cambacérès, to draft a comprehensive civil code.

The Napoleonic Code introduced several groundbreaking principles that continue to shape modern legal systems:

- **Clarity and Simplicity:** The code aimed to provide a clear and concise set of laws, doing away with the complexity and ambiguity characteristic of the feudal legal systems of the time. It prioritized simplicity and accessibility, making the law comprehensible to the common citizen.
- **Equality before the Law:** This code emphasized the principle of equality, stating that all citizens were equal before the law. This was a significant departure from the privileges and inequalities that had characterized the Ancien Régime.
- **Property Rights**: It protected private property rights, reinforcing the idea that individuals had a right to possess, use, and dispose of their property as they saw fit. This provision was influential in the development of capitalist economies.
- **Freedom of Contract:** The Napoleonic Code supported freedom of contract, allowing individuals to enter into agreements based on their own volition. This laid the foundation for modern contract law.
- **Family Law**: The code reformed family law by allowing divorce, granting fathers greater authority over their children, and simplifying inheritance rules.

In addition to the Napoleonic Code, Napoleon's rule in France was marked by wide-ranging reforms that transformed the country in various ways:

- **Educational Reforms:** Napoleon recognized the importance of education in building a strong nation. He established a public education system known as the Napoleonic University, which provided education from elementary to university levels. This system aimed to produce skilled bureaucrats and professionals.
- **Administrative Reforms:** To streamline governance, Napoleon centralized administrative power. He divided France into departments, each with a prefect appointed by the central government. This structure improved efficiency and control.
- **Legal Reforms:** Beyond the Napoleonic Code, legal reforms included the establishment of the Council of State, which acted as a legal advisory body and helped standardize laws and regulations.
- **Financial Reforms:** Napoleon stabilized France's finances by introducing the franc as the national currency and establishing the Bank of France. These measures contributed to economic stability.
- **Religious Reforms:** Napoleon signed the Concordat with the Catholic Church in 1801, reconciling state and church relations. While Catholicism was recognized as the dominant religion, religious freedom was guaranteed.

The Napoleonic Code and the wide-ranging reforms instituted by Napoleon in France represent a significant turning point in legal, social, and administrative history. These reforms modernized France and had a lasting influence on other countries and legal systems worldwide. The principles of equality, clarity, and rationality in the Napoleonic Code continue to shape modern legal systems, emphasizing the enduring legacy of Napoleon's era of reform.

42. Austerlitz: Napoleon's Greatest Victory

On December 2nd, 1805, the Battle of Austerlitz, fought between the French army led by Emperor Napoleon Bonaparte and the combined forces of the Russian Empire and the Holy Roman Empire, unfolded on the icy plains near the town of Austerlitz in what is now the Czech Republic. This battle is often regarded as Napoleon's greatest military triumph, showcasing his tactical brilliance and earning him the title of a military genius.

To appreciate the significance of Austerlitz, it's essential to understand the strategic backdrop of the Napoleonic Wars. In 1805, the Third Coalition, comprising Russia, Austria, and the United Kingdom, had formed with the aim of defeating Napoleon's French Empire, which had been expanding rapidly across Europe. The Allies planned to encircle and crush Napoleon's Grande Armée, setting the stage for the Battle of Austerlitz.

Napoleon recognized the danger posed by the superior numbers of the Allied armies. He initiated a strategic retreat to lure them into a vulnerable position, drawing the Allies deeper into France. This maneuver gave him time to consolidate his forces and choose the battlefield. Napoleon selected the Pratzen Heights near Austerlitz as the battleground. He realized that these heights held the key to victory. He deliberately weakened his right flank to draw the Allies into a decisive confrontation, making it appear vulnerable. A thick fog covered the battlefield on the morning of the battle, obscuring visibility. Napoleon recognized this as an advantage and waited until the fog lifted, preventing the Allies from fully assessing his forces' disposition.

Believing Napoleon's right flank was weak, the Allies launched a massive assault on that sector. However, this played into Napoleon's hands, as he had concentrated his forces in the center and left. Napoleon ordered a devastating counterattack as the Allies committed their forces to the attack. The French infantry, under Marshal Soult, assaulted the weakened Allied center, splitting their forces in two. Meanwhile, Marshal Davout held the Pratzen Heights with a smaller force. His tenacity and the foggy conditions delayed the Allies' realization that the heights had not been abandoned. Once the fog cleared, it was too late, and Napoleon's forces held the crucial high ground.

The Battle of Austerlitz ended in a resounding victory for Napoleon. The Allies suffered heavy casualties and were forced to retreat. This triumph not only solidified Napoleon's reputation as a military genius but also led to the signing of the Treaty of Pressburg, which greatly favored France and dismantled the Holy Roman Empire. Austerlitz marked the pinnacle of Napoleon's military career.

43. Napoleon's Russian Catastrophe: The Retreat from Moscow

The retreat from Moscow in 1812 stands as one of the most catastrophic and infamous episodes in military history. Emperor Napoleon Bonaparte, who had once been the master of Europe, led his Grande Armée into Russia with grand ambitions of conquest. However, as the Russian campaign unfolded, it became clear that it would be a brutal and ultimately disastrous endeavor.

By 1812, Napoleon's French Empire was at its zenith. With most of Europe under his control, he sought to expand his influence in Russia. His ambition was to compel the Russian Tsar, Alexander I, to adhere to the Continental System, an economic blockade against British trade. For this, Napoleon assembled a colossal army, often referred to as the Grande Armée, consisting of over 600,000 soldiers from various European nations under his control. In June 1812, they crossed the Neman River and entered Russian territory.

The Russian army, under Field Marshal Mikhail Kutuzov, opted to engage Napoleon at the Battle of Borodino in September 1812. This brutal conflict was one of the bloodiest of the Napoleonic Wars, with heavy casualties. While the French emerged victorious, their losses were staggering. After the costly battle, Napoleon's forces entered Moscow in September 1812. However, the Russian army had employed a scorched-earth strategy, leaving the city abandoned and in flames. Napoleon had no choice but to occupy a ruined, depopulated Moscow. As winter descended upon Russia, the situation for the French grew dire. The harsh Russian winter, coupled with dwindling supplies and the vast distances they had to traverse, took a heavy toll on Napoleon's army.

Realizing that remaining in Moscow was unsustainable, Napoleon ordered the retreat in late October 1812. This retreat would prove to be a nightmarish ordeal. The Grande Armée faced extreme hardships during the retreat. Starvation, frostbite, and constant harassment by Russian forces further depleted their numbers. Thousands perished from exhaustion and hunger. One of the most desperate moments came at the Bérézina River in November 1812. The French had to cross the freezing river while under relentless Russian attacks. Many drowned or were killed during this crossing.

By the time Napoleon and his shattered army crossed back into friendly territory, only a fraction of the once-mighty Grande Armée remained. Estimates of casualties vary, but it is believed that only around 10% of the invading force survived. The retreat from Moscow marked a turning point in Napoleon's fortunes. The catastrophic losses severely weakened his grip on Europe, and it marked the beginning of his eventual downfall. The disaster in Russia galvanized the other European powers against Napoleon. A Sixth Coalition was formed, and a series of campaigns known as the War of the Sixth Coalition would ultimately lead to Napoleon's defeat and exile.

44. Waterloo: The End of an Era

The Battle of Waterloo, fought on June 18th, 1815, near the town of Waterloo in present-day Belgium, stands as a pivotal moment in history. It marked the culmination of a series of conflicts known as the Napoleonic Wars and, more significantly, the end of an era dominated by one of history's most iconic figures, Emperor Napoleon Bonaparte. This epic battle pitted the French forces under Napoleon against the combined armies of the Seventh Coalition, led by the Duke of Wellington and Prussian Field Marshal Gebhard Leberecht von Blücher.

Napoleon's defeat in Russia encouraged the formation of the Sixth Coalition, comprising Britain, Russia, Prussia, and Austria. The Coalition launched a successful campaign in 1814 that culminated in the capture of Paris. Facing pressure from his marshals and a lack of support, Napoleon abdicated on April 6th, 1814. He was exiled to the island of Elba, and Louis XVIII was restored to the French throne. Napoleon's exile was short-lived. On February 26th, 1815, he escaped from Elba and returned to France. This event marked the beginning of the Hundred Days when he reclaimed power and declared himself Emperor again.

Napoleon moved swiftly to raise a new army and launch a pre-emptive strike against the coalition forces assembling in Belgium. His strategy was to divide and defeat the allied armies before they could unite. On June 16th, 1815, Napoleon engaged the Prussian army under Blücher at the Battle of Ligny. The French emerged victorious, but the Prussians managed an organized retreat, setting the stage for critical development. Simultaneously, a minor engagement occurred at Quatre Bras, where the French sought to prevent the British under Wellington from linking up with the Prussians. It ended inconclusively.

On June 18th, 1815, the main confrontation occurred at Waterloo. Wellington had chosen a defensive position anchored on the farmhouse of Hougoumont and the ridge at Mont St. Jean. His forces were positioned on the high ground. Napoleon launched a series of attacks on the British lines throughout the day, including a massive assault on Hougoumont. The British, supported by the arrival of Prussian reinforcements under Blücher, held their ground despite heavy casualties. In the late afternoon, Prussian forces arrived in force, threatening Napoleon's right flank. This development forced Napoleon into a desperate last-ditch attack on Wellington's center. The attack on Wellington's center failed, and the French army began to disintegrate. Realizing the battle was lost, Napoleon ordered a retreat.

Napoleon's defeat at Waterloo marked the end of his rule and ambitions. He was exiled to the remote island of Saint Helena in the South Atlantic, where he spent the remainder of his life. The defeat of Napoleon at Waterloo led to the Congress of Vienna, where the European powers sought to redraw the map of Europe and restore order after the upheaval of the Napoleonic Wars. Louis XVIII was restored to the French throne, marking the return of the Bourbon Monarchy.

45. Napoleon's Influence on Modern Europe

Napoleon Bonaparte, one of history's most iconic figures, left an unforgettable mark on Europe that continues to shape the continent's political, social, and cultural landscape to this day. Firstly, it's crucial to acknowledge the undeniable impact of Napoleon's military conquests and reforms on modern Europe. His ambitious campaigns, which extended French control over vast swathes of the continent, not only redrew national boundaries but also introduced a series of reforms that modernized European societies. The Napoleonic Code, for instance, remains a cornerstone of legal systems in several European countries, emphasizing principles of equality before the law, property rights, and secularism. These principles continue to underpin modern legal systems across Europe.

Furthermore, Napoleon's military innovations, including the concept of the citizen army, have had a lasting impact on modern military strategy and tactics. The idea of a conscripted national army became a standard model in Europe and beyond, reshaping the nature of warfare and the relationship between states and their citizens. However, opinions about Napoleon's influence on modern Europe are not solely positive. Critics argue that his militaristic ambitions and expansionist policies led to widespread suffering and loss of life across the continent. The Napoleonic Wars, which spanned over a decade, brought devastation to countless regions and left a legacy of conflict and instability in their wake. Skeptics contend that Napoleon's drive for power disrupted the delicate balance of power in Europe and sowed the seeds for future conflicts, including the two World Wars.

Moreover, Napoleon's impact on national identities in Europe is a subject of debate. While he contributed to the spread of nationalist sentiment in some regions by redrawing boundaries and creating new political entities, he also imposed French cultural norms and institutions on conquered territories. This has led some to argue that his legacy is one of both nation-building and cultural imperialism, with mixed consequences for modern European identities.

In terms of governance, Napoleon's autocratic rule and his establishment of client states have raised questions about the balance between centralized authority and local autonomy. His administrative reforms have been praised for streamlining government functions and modernizing institutions, but they have also been criticized for concentrating power in the hands of the state.

Chapter 10: Stories of Adolf Hitler

Adolf Hitler, a name that still sends shivers down the spine of history, is undeniably one of the most polarizing and consequential figures of the 20th century. Often regarded as the person who altered the course of world history in a way no one could have anticipated, Hitler's impact is both a chilling reminder of the darkest depths humanity can reach and a cautionary tale for generations to come. You can't study European history without coming across Hitler; maybe you've heard "Heil Hitler!" echo through the annals of time, or perhaps the word "Führer" has crossed your path. Hitler's rise to power, marked by his magnetic charisma and ruthlessly efficient political maneuvering, ultimately led to a cataclysmic clash of ideologies that resulted in unimaginable suffering and global conflict.

Adolf Hitler, a name that still sends shivers down the spine of history.

46. The Making of a Dictator: Hitler's Early Years

Adolf Hitler was born on April 20th, 1889, in Braunau am Inn, Austria-Hungary, to Alois Hitler and Klara Pölzl. His childhood was marked by both joys and hardships. Alois Hitler was a stern and occasionally abusive father, while Klara was a gentle and nurturing mother. Young Adolf displayed a talent for drawing but struggled academically. His family moved frequently during his childhood, and he attended several schools in Austria and Germany. This constant upheaval made it challenging for him to form lasting friendships.

From a young age, Hitler showed a talent for drawing, and he harbored dreams of becoming an artist. His early exposure to art came from his mother, Klara, who supported his artistic pursuits and encouraged his creativity. Young Adolf frequently sketched landscapes, buildings, and portraits, often focusing on architectural scenes. In 1907, at the age of 18, Hitler moved to Vienna with the hope of attending the Vienna Academy of Fine Arts, a prestigious institution for aspiring artists. However, his dreams of gaining admission were shattered when he failed the entrance exam. This rejection was a significant blow to his self-esteem and aspirations as an artist.

Life in Vienna during this period was challenging for Hitler. He lived in poverty, eking out a meager existence by selling postcards of his artwork and living in homeless shelters. He often frequented museums and art galleries, where he developed a deep admiration for classical German and Austrian art. It was during his time in Vienna that Hitler began to develop strong nationalistic and anti-Semitic views. He became deeply influenced by the prevalent anti-Semitic rhetoric of the time, and these ideas would later become a central part of his political ideology.

While Hitler continued to produce art throughout his life, his works were met with limited success. His artistic style was primarily focused on landscapes, scenes of architecture, and portraits. His paintings often lacked the innovative and experimental qualities that were gaining popularity in the art world during the early 20th century. Hitler's inability to gain recognition as an artist, combined with his growing disillusionment with life in Vienna, fueled his sense of resentment and bitterness. He began to view himself as a misunderstood genius whose talents had been unfairly ignored.

As World War I erupted in 1914, Hitler saw an opportunity to leave his unfulfilling artistic career behind and enlist as a soldier. His service in the war would prove to be a turning point in his life, leading him down the path of political radicalization and ultimately to the rise of the Nazi Party. In retrospect, Hitler's failure to establish himself as an artist was a crucial factor in his transformation into a dictator. His artistic struggles, combined with his disillusionment with Vienna and his experiences as a soldier in World War I, laid the groundwork for his later political ambitions. The rejection he faced as an artist left him with a deep-seated desire for recognition and power, which he would ultimately seek to fulfill through his political career.

Hitler's experiences as a soldier during World War I would have a profound impact on his worldview. He served as a frontline soldier in the trenches of the Western Front and participated in several significant battles. One of the most notable events occurred during the Battle of the Somme (1916) when he was wounded twice. First, he was injured by a shell blast and later suffered the effects of mustard gas, which temporarily blinded him. During his time in the military, Hitler received the Iron Cross, Second Class, for his bravery and dedication. Despite his wounds, he remained committed to the German cause and saw the war as a noble struggle.

However, it was the outcome of World War I that deeply scarred Hitler. The news of Germany's defeat and the signing of the Armistice in 1918 devastated him. He, like many others, believed that Germany had been betrayed by politicians and blamed Jews, communists, and perceived internal enemies for the nation's downfall.

47. The Beer Hall Putsch: An Attempt at Revolution

As World War I came to an end, Adolf Hitler faced an uncertain future. His dreams of becoming an artist had long since withered in the face of his experiences as a soldier and the harsh realities of post-war Germany. The trauma of the war and his deep resentment towards the Weimar Republic fueled a growing ambition within him. The defeated and demoralized Germany of the early 1920s provided fertile ground for extremist ideologies to take root. Having tasted the intoxicating allure of leadership during his military service, Hitler began to see himself as a savior of Germany, a man with a mission to restore the nation to its former glory.

As he returned to civilian life, he turned his attention toward politics. On the evening of November 8th, 1923, Munich was enveloped in darkness as Adolf Hitler and his band of fervent followers gathered at the Bürgerbräukeller beer hall. Little did the city know that this seemingly ordinary night would witness an audacious coup attempt, known as the Beer Hall Putsch, which would shape the course of history. That evening, Hitler and approximately 2,000 of his loyal supporters organized a rally at the Bürgerbräukeller beer hall to protest the Weimar government and its perceived failings, particularly its handling of the Ruhr Crisis and the economic strife facing the German people.

The atmosphere became increasingly charged with revolutionary fervor as Hitler delivered a fiery speech. He proclaimed the imminent overthrow of the Weimar Republic and the establishment of a "national government." He was joined by prominent figures of the Nazi Party, including Ernst Röhm and Rudolf Hess, both of whom played significant roles in the events that followed. Inspired by Hitler's impassioned speech, the Nazi paramilitary group, the SA (Sturmabteilung), set off on the night of November 8th to seize key government buildings in Munich. Their aim was to force the Bavarian government to join their cause and then march on Berlin to topple the Weimar government.

The Putsch was, however, a hastily planned operation. As the SA members marched through the streets of Munich, they encountered a police blockade at the Feldherrnhalle, a memorial to Bavarian military heroes. A brief but intense firefight ensued. The police quickly overwhelmed the disorganized and ill-equipped SA troops. In the midst of the chaos, Hitler was injured by a stray bullet – dislocating his shoulder. He was subsequently arrested and taken into custody. The Beer Hall Putsch had failed spectacularly as 16 Nazis and four police officers were killed in the skirmish, while many others, including Hitler, were injured. The Weimar government remained firmly in control, and the Nazi Party was banned.

Adolf Hitler and his co-conspirators were put on trial for treason in February 1924. The trial provided Hitler with a high-profile platform to espouse his nationalist and anti-Semitic views, effectively turning the courtroom into a propaganda stage. During the trial, Hitler expressed no remorse for his actions and instead defended his motivations, portraying himself as a patriot. The sympathetic judge handed down a relatively lenient sentence of five years in prison, of which Hitler would serve only nine months. During his incarceration at Landsberg Prison, Hitler penned his infamous autobiography and political manifesto, "Mein Kampf."

While the Beer Hall Putsch appeared to be a failure initially, it had several profound consequences. Firstly, it catapulted Hitler and the Nazi Party into the national spotlight, allowing them to reach a broader audience with their extremist ideology. Secondly, Hitler's trial and imprisonment allowed him to consolidate his ideas, refine his propaganda, and solidify his leadership within the Nazi Party. He emerged from prison with a renewed determination to achieve power through legal means.

48. Hitler's Rise to Power: Exploiting a Nation's Despair

Adolf Hitler's ascent to power in Germany was a testament to his ability to exploit the grievances and fears of a nation reeling from the aftermath of World War I and the economic hardships of the Weimar Republic. Following his release from prison after the failed Beer Hall Putsch in 1923, Hitler embarked on a calculated and strategic path that would lead him to the chancellorship of Germany in 1933. When Hitler was released from prison in December 1924, Germany was grappling with numerous issues that left its citizens disillusioned and discontented. The Treaty of Versailles imposed heavy reparations and territorial losses, leading to economic turmoil, hyperinflation, and widespread unemployment. The Weimar Republic, plagued by political instability and coalition governments, struggled to address these challenges effectively.

After the failure of the Beer Hall Putsch, Hitler realized that a violent coup was not the most viable path to power. He resolved to achieve his goals legally through elections and political maneuvering. Hitler's gift for charismatic and impassioned speeches became a potent weapon. He could tap into the frustrations and fears of the German people, promising them a way out of their suffering. Hitler recognized the power of propaganda in shaping public opinion. He established the Nazi Party's newspaper, "Völkischer Beobachter," and employed Joseph Goebbels to mastermind the dissemination of Nazi propaganda. After the Putsch, the Nazi Party was banned. Hitler worked to rebuild it, drawing in new supporters and expanding its base. The SA, or Brownshirts, served as a paramilitary force that intimidated political opponents.

During the late 1920s and early 1930s, the Nazi Party gained increasing support through a combination of factors. Hitler and the Nazis strategically adapted their message to appeal to a wide range of voters, from nationalists and disaffected veterans to the economically disadvantaged. The frequent collapse of coalition governments, coupled with the inability to address economic problems effectively, disillusioned many Germans with democratic governance. In the July 1930 Reichstag elections, the Nazi Party became the second-largest political party in Germany, securing 18.3% of the vote. This electoral success gave Hitler a prominent position in the political landscape.

In January 1933, following a series of backroom deals and political maneuvering, President Paul von Hindenburg appointed Hitler as Chancellor of Germany. The decision was driven by a belief among conservative politicians that they could control Hitler and that he would provide stability. Hitler's appointment marked the beginning of the end for the Weimar Republic and the erosion of German democracy. He moved quickly to consolidate power, using the Reichstag Fire in February 1933 as a pretext to push through the Reichstag Fire Decree, which suspended civil liberties and allowed for the arrest of political opponents.

Hitler's regime was characterized by its totalitarian control over every aspect of German life. The Nazis suppressed dissent through the brutal secret police, the Gestapo, and silenced opposition through censorship and propaganda. They indoctrinated youth through the Hitler Youth organization and redefined education to align with Nazi ideology. The Nuremberg Laws of 1935 stripped Jews of their rights, segregating them from the rest of society.

One of the most horrifying aspects of Hitler's rule was the Holocaust, a systematic genocide targeting Jews and other minority groups. The Nazis established extermination camps like Auschwitz, Sobibor, and Treblinka, where millions were systematically murdered. The Holocaust resulted in the deaths of six million Jews and millions of others, including Romani people, disabled individuals, and political dissidents. Hitler's fanatical anti-Semitism fueled this unparalleled atrocity. The Holocaust remains a haunting testament to the depths of human cruelty.

Entire families were annihilated, and communities were destroyed. The survivors bore lifelong scars, and the trauma of the Holocaust continues to reverberate through generations.

Hitler's expansionist ambitions led to the outbreak of World War II in 1939 when Germany invaded Poland. The war escalated, engulfing Europe and later expanding to other continents. Hitler's military campaigns, including the Blitzkrieg tactics, the invasion of France, and the Eastern Front, resulted in millions of deaths and widespread devastation. The impact of World War II was catastrophic. Cities were reduced to rubble, economies were shattered, and millions of lives were lost. The war's consequences extended far beyond Europe, affecting nations worldwide.

49. Operation Barbarossa: The Turning Point

Operation Barbarossa, launched by Nazi Germany on June 22nd, 1941, marked a pivotal moment in World War II. This massive military campaign, driven by Adolf Hitler's ambitions, saw Germany invade the Soviet Union with the aim of securing Lebensraum (living space) and crippling the Soviet state. While initially successful, the operation ultimately became a turning point in the war due to several key factors. Operation Barbarossa was one of the largest military campaigns in history. It involved three million German soldiers, supported by hundreds of thousands of vehicles and over 3,000 aircraft. The sheer scale and ambition of the invasion demonstrated Hitler's determination to achieve a swift victory over the Soviet Union.

In the early months of the campaign, German forces made significant advances into Soviet territory. They captured vast swaths of land, inflicted heavy casualties on the Red Army, and encircled and captured hundreds of thousands of Soviet soldiers. Key cities like Kyiv and Smolensk fell to the Germans, and the Soviet Union appeared to be on the brink of collapse. However, Operation Barbarossa faced severe logistical challenges. The vast distances of the Soviet Union stretched German supply lines, making it increasingly difficult to sustain the rapid advance. Harsh weather conditions, particularly the brutal Russian winter, exacerbated the logistical woes. German soldiers lacked adequate winter clothing and equipment, leading to frostbite and low morale.

As the German advance slowed due to logistical difficulties and stubborn Soviet resistance, it became evident that the Red Army was far from defeated. The Soviets displayed remarkable resilience and adaptability. They adopted a strategy of scorched-earth tactics, denying the Germans valuable resources as they retreated eastward. The vastness of the Soviet Union allowed for strategic depth, and the Soviets regrouped and launched counteroffensives.

The Battle of Stalingrad, fought from August 23rd, 1942, to February 2nd, 1943, marked a critical turning point in Operation Barbarossa. The city of Stalingrad became a symbol of Soviet resistance, and both sides suffered immense casualties in the brutal street-by-street combat. The Soviets eventually encircled the German Sixth Army, leading to its surrender in February 1943. The loss of the Sixth Army, along with its equipment and personnel, was a devastating blow to the German war effort.

By 1943, Operation Barbarossa had stalled. The Germans faced a protracted war of attrition on the Eastern Front, with neither side able to gain a decisive advantage. Additionally, the Soviet Union's growing strength, aided by lend-lease supplies from the Western Allies, further tilted the balance in favor of the Soviets.

Operation Barbarossa, initially perceived as a campaign of swift victory, had become a quagmire for the Germans. By late 1943 and early 1944, the Soviets had regained much of their lost territory and were advancing into Eastern Europe. The successful Soviet offensives, including the Battles of Kursk and Bagration, had decisively shifted the momentum of the war. Operation Barbarossa had not achieved its objectives. Instead, it triggered a protracted and costly conflict with the Soviet Union. It marked the beginning of a long retreat for the German army, culminating in the capture of Berlin by Soviet forces in April 1945.

50. The Führer's End: Hitler's Downfall and the Death of Nazism

As the Allies closed in on Germany from both the west and east, the situation on the Eastern Front was particularly dire. The Soviet Red Army, having gained immense strength and momentum, was advancing rapidly. By early 1945, they had entered German territory, capturing key cities like Warsaw and reaching the Oder River, just miles from Berlin. In January 1945, Hitler retreated to his underground bunker in Berlin, known as the Führerbunker. This reinforced complex, located beneath the Reich Chancellery, became the epicenter of Nazi power in the final months of the war. It was here that Hitler and his closest associates, including Eva Braun and Joseph Goebbels, would make their last stand.

Hitler's mental state had deteriorated significantly by this point. He clung to delusional hopes of a miraculous turnaround and continued to issue irrational orders to non-existent armies. He rejected any notion of surrender and vowed to fight to the death. As the Soviet Red Army encircled Berlin in April 1945, the city endured a ferocious and devastating battle. The fighting was characterized by street-to-street combat, heavy artillery bombardments, and widespread destruction. Civilians suffered immensely, and the city's infrastructure crumbled.

In the midst of this chaos, Hitler married Eva Braun on April 29, 1945, in the Führerbunker. The following day, they both committed suicide. Hitler took his own life by swallowing a cyanide capsule and shooting himself in the head, while Eva Braun also ingested poison. Their bodies were later discovered in the bunker. With Berlin under Soviet control and its leaders dead, the remnants of the Nazi regime had no choice but to surrender. On May 7th, 1945, General Alfred Jodl signed the unconditional surrender of all German forces in Reims, France, which came into effect on May 8th, 1945, officially marking the end of World War II in Europe.

The death of Adolf Hitler and the surrender of Nazi Germany brought an end to one of the darkest chapters in history. The horrors of the Holocaust, the devastation wrought by the war, and the scale of human suffering were brought to light as Allied forces liberated concentration camps and occupied German territory. In the aftermath of the war, the leaders of Nazi Germany, including those who had survived and been captured, were brought to justice at the Nuremberg Trials. These trials, held from November 20th, 1945, to October 1st, 1946, prosecuted individuals responsible for war crimes, crimes against humanity, and other atrocities committed during the war.

Conclusion

As you turn the last page of this book, take a moment to appreciate the significance of the narratives you've read about and their lasting impact on the present day. This exploration reminds you of the diverse history that has shaped the continent and continues to influence Europe and the wider world. You've learned all about the epochs of Europe's past, from the awe-inspiring civilizations of Greece and Rome, with their monumental contributions to philosophy, art, and governance, to the tumultuous waves of the Middle Ages, where knights, kings, and peasants each played their part in forging the continent's destiny. You can only marvel at the explosion of creativity during the Renaissance and witnessed the profound transformations brought about by the Enlightenment, an era that championed reason, liberty, and equality.

Throughout these stories, you've also come across individuals whose actions and ideas have reverberated through the ages. From the revolutionary thoughts of Voltaire and Rousseau to the courage of the human rights rebellions, these individuals have left a mark on the course of European history that cannot be erased. However, this learning isn't solely supposed to be an exploration of the past; it serves as a bridge to understanding the present and the future. Europe's history is a living testament to the enduring consequences of past actions. The echoes of empire-building, the lessons learned from devastating wars, and the struggles for democracy and human rights all continue to shape the continent's societies and institutions.

In today's Europe, the product of centuries of interactions, conflicts, and collaborations can be witnessed. The European Union, an entity born from the ashes of World War II, symbolizes Europe's commitment to unity and cooperation, driven by the imperative to prevent another catastrophic conflict. Understanding these stories in their contemporary context is essential. Europe's history is not a distant relic but an ever-present force shaping today's societies, politics, and collective memory. In this increasingly interconnected world, where actions in one part of the globe can have far-reaching consequences, the lessons of history are more vital than ever.

European history isn't just a collection of stories; it's a living legacy that continues to shape the world today. These narratives should inspire you to learn from the past, foster empathy and understanding, and work towards a future that values diversity, champions peace, and upholds the ideals of justice and progress.

Check out another book in the series

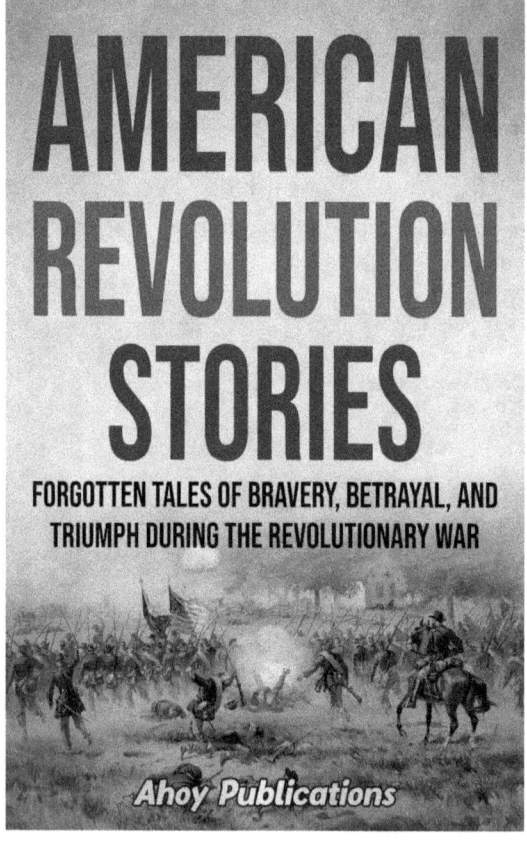

References

(n.d.). Wordpress.Com. https://mrcaseyhistory.files.wordpress.com/2019/02/vikings-raiders-or-traders.pdf

(N.d.-a). Uchicago.edu. https://penelope.uchicago.edu/~grout/encyclopaedia_romana/miscellanea/cleopatra/egypt.html#:~:text=Julius%20Caesar%20defeated%20Ptolemy%20XII,XIII%20on%20the%20Egyptian%20throne.

(N.d.-b). Historyofinformation.com. https://www.historyofinformation.com/detail.php?entryid=3337

1769-1793: Napoleon Bonaparte's early years. (n.d.). Napoleon.org. https://www.napoleon.org/en/history-of-the-two-empires/timelines/1769-1793-napoleon-bonapartes-early-years/

Adolf Hitler: Rise to power, impact & death. (2009, October 29). HISTORY. https://www.history.com/topics/world-war-ii/adolf-hitler-1

Anastasi, L. (2023, April 23). The Siege of Paris: City Under Fire. Medieval History – Yesterday in a Nutshell. https://historymedieval.com/the-siege-of-paris-city-under-fire/

Ancient Greek Democracy. (2018, August 23). HISTORY. https://www.history.com/topics/ancient-greece/ancient-greece-democracy

Beer hall putsch. (2009, November 9). HISTORY. https://www.history.com/topics/european-history/beer-hall-putsch

Bertocchi, G. (2016). The legacies of slavery in and out of Africa. IZA Journal of Migration, 5(1). https://doi.org/10.1186/s40176-016-0072-0

Beware the Ides of March: Julius Caesar's assassination in art. (n.d.). Artuk.org. https://artuk.org/discover/stories/beware-the-ides-of-march-julius-caesars-assassination-in-art

Birth of the Vikings. (n.d.). Sky HISTORY TV Channel. https://www.history.co.uk/shows/vikings/articles/birth-of-the-vikings

Black Death – Bubonic Plague, Europe, 1347. (n.d.). In Encyclopedia Britannica.

British Library. (n.d.). Www.Bl.UK ; The British Library.

British Library. (n.d.). Www.Bl.UK ; The British Library

Caesar crosses the Rubicon. (n.d.). Nationalgeographic.org. https://education.nationalgeographic.org/resource/caesar-crosses-rubicon/

Campbell, E. M. J., & Fernandez-Armesto, F. (2023). Vasco da Gama. In Encyclopedia Britannica.

Cartwright, M. (2016). Pizarro & the Fall of the Inca Empire. World History Encyclopedia. https://www.worldhistory.org/article/915/pizarro--the-fall-of-the-inca-empire/

Cartwright, M. (2020). Peasants' Revolt. World History Encyclopedia.

Cartwright, M. (2021). Vasco da Gama. World History Encyclopedia. https://www.worldhistory.org/Vasco_da_Gama/

Cartwright, M. (2023). Athenian Democracy. World History Encyclopedia. https://www.worldhistory.org/Athenian_Democracy/

Cartwright, M. (2023). Black Death. World History Encyclopedia. https://www.worldhistory.org/Black_Death/

Chintaluri, A., & Chintaluri, A. (2022, April 18). The Ancient Agora of Athens – Everything you Need to Know to Plan a Visit [Video]. Headout Blog. https://www.headout.com/blog/agora-of-athens/

Christopher Columbus Reaches the "New World." (2009, November 24). HISTORY. https://www.history.com/this-day-in-history/columbus-reaches-the-new-world

Christopher Columbus. (2009, November 9). HISTORY. https://www.history.com/topics/exploration/christopher-columbus

Columbus Lands in South America. (2010, July 21). HISTORY. https://www.history.com/this-day-in-history/columbus-lands-in-south-america

Constitutional Rights Foundation. (n.d.). Crf-usa.org. https://www.crf-usa.org/bill-of-rights-in-action/bria-26-2-the-black-death-a-catastrophe-in-medieval-europe.html

Decameron web. (n.d.-a). Brown.edu. https://www.brown.edu/Departments/Italian_Studies/dweb/plague/effects/social.php

Decameron web. (n.d.-b). Brown.edu.
https://www.brown.edu/Departments/Italian_Studies/dweb/plague/effects/social.php

Dow, D. (n.d.). Who killed Julius Caesar & why was he betrayed? Magellantv.com. https://www.magellantv.com/articles/who-killed-julius-caesar-why-was-he-betrayed

French revolutionaries storm the Bastille. (2009, November 24). HISTORY. https://www.history.com/this-day-in-history/french-revolutionaries-storm-bastille

Garcia, B. (2018). Romulus and Remus. World History Encyclopedia. https://www.worldhistory.org/Romulus_and_Remus/

Gill, N. (2018). Ecclesia, the Greek Assembly. ThoughtCo. https://www.thoughtco.com/ecclesia-assembly-of-athens-118833

Greece; The Pros and Cons of Democracy Therein – 2680 Words | Bartleby. (n.d.). https://www.bartleby.com/essay/Greece-The-Pros-and-Cons-of-Democracy-P3MAPS83DRVA

Greek City-States. (n.d.). https://education.nationalgeographic.org/resource/greek-city-states/

Greenspan, J. (2012, June 22). Why was Napoleon's invasion of Russia the beginning of the end? HISTORY. https://www.history.com/news/napoleons-disastrous-invasion-of-russia

History & Policy. (n.d.). History & Policy. https://www.historyandpolicy.org/policy-papers/papers/the-economic-consequences-of-plague-lessons-for-the-age-of-covid-19

Holmes, R. C. L. (2021, January 16). The Gallic Wars: How Julius Caesar conquered Gaul (modern France). TheCollector. https://www.thecollector.com/gallic-wars-how-julius-caesar-conquered-gaul/

How did Julius Caesar rise to power? (n.d.). Ipl.org. https://www.ipl.org/essay/How-Did-Julius-Caesar-Rise-To-Power-PC9XYVHT8SM

Hudson, M. (2023). Battle of Tenochtitlán. In Encyclopedia Britannica.

Introduction to Kant's "What Is Enlightenment?" (n.d.). K-State.Edu. https://www.k-state.edu/english/baker/english233/Kant-WIE-intro.htm

Jarus, O. (2020, March 11). Lindisfarne: The "Holy Island" where Vikings spilled the "blood of saints." Livescience.Com; Live Science. https://www.livescience.com/lindisfarne.html

Johnson, N., Koyama, M., & Jedwab, R. (n.d.). Pandemics, places, and populations: Evidence from the Black Death. CEPR. https://cepr.org/voxeu/columns/pandemics-places-and-populations-evidence-black-death

Julius Caesar Crosses the Rubicon, 49 BC. (n.d.). Eyewitnesstohistory.com.
http://www.eyewitnesstohistory.com/caesar.htm

How the First Triumvirate changed ancient Rome. (n.d.). History Skills.
https://www.historyskills.com/classroom/ancient-history/anc-1st-triumvirate-reading/

Wasson, D. L. (2016). First Triumvirate. World History Encyclopedia.
https://www.worldhistory.org/First_Triumvirate/

Julius Caesar. (n.d.). Nationalgeographic.org.
https://education.nationalgeographic.org/resource/julius-caesar/

Julius Caesar's rise to power and dictatorship. (2022, September 15).
Edubirdie. https://edubirdie.com/examples/julius-caesars-rise-to-power-and-dictatorship/

Lesso, R. (2022). What Were the City States of Ancient Greece?
TheCollector. https://www.thecollector.com/what-were-the-city-states-of-ancient-greece/

Life and Teachings of Jesus. (n.d.). Pluralism.Org. https://pluralism.org/life-and-teachings-of-jesus

Little, B. (2023, July 13). Cleopatra's complicated inner circle: Siblings,
successors, and lovers. HISTORY. https://www.history.com/news/cleopatras-complicated-inner-circle-siblings-successors-and-lovers

Lochun, K. (2020, December 21). Who were the Kievan Rus, and what do
they have to do with the Vikings? HistoryExtra.
https://www.historyextra.com/period/viking/rus-vikings-kievan-rus-rurik-vladimir-great/

Marco, S. (2023, March 14). Caesar and Cleopatra in Egypt.
Odysseytraveller.com; Odyssey Traveller.
https://www.odysseytraveller.com/articles/caesar-and-cleopatra-in-egypt/

Mark, H. W. (2023). Battle of Austerlitz. World History Encyclopedia.
https://www.worldhistory.org/article/2253/battle-of-austerlitz/

Mark, J. J. (2018). Kievan Rus. World History Encyclopedia.
https://www.worldhistory.org/Kievan_Rus/

Mark, J. J. (2020). Effects of the Black Death on Europe. World History
Encyclopedia. https://www.worldhistory.org/article/1543/effects-of-the-black-death-on-europe/

Martinez, J. (2023). The Medici Family: Ultimate Power and Legacy In The
Renaissance. TheCollector. https://www.thecollector.com/the-medici-family-legacy/

McLean, J. (n.d.-a). Napoleon's defeat at Waterloo. Lumenlearning.com.
https://courses.lumenlearning.com/suny-hccc-worldhistory2/chapter/napoleons-defeat-at-waterloo/

McLean, J. (n.d.-b). The Napoleonic code. Lumenlearning.com. https://courses.lumenlearning.com/suny-hccc-worldhistory2/chapter/the-napoleonic-code/

Medievalists.net. (2023, July 18). How Christianity came to Medieval Europe. Medievalists.Net. https://www.medievalists.net/2023/07/christianity-medieval-europe/

Moya, M. J. (2022, March 17). Saint Patrick, the man behind the St. Patrick's Day holiday, wasn't even Irish. USA Today. https://www.usatoday.com/story/news/2022/03/17/st-patrick-day-saint/7039195001/

Napoleon Bonaparte. (2009, November 9). HISTORY. https://www.history.com/topics/european-history/napoleon

Napoleon Bonaparte. (2020, October 11). BYJUS; BYJU'S. https://byjus.com/free-ias-prep/napoleon-bonaparte/

Napoleon invades Russia. (n.d.). Nationalgeographic.org. https://education.nationalgeographic.org/resource/napoleon-invades-russia/

Napoleonic Code approved in France. (2010, February 9). HISTORY. https://www.history.com/this-day-in-history/napoleonic-code-approved-in-france

ODYSSEY/Rome. (n.d.). Emory.edu. https://carlos.emory.edu/htdocs/ODYSSEY/ROME/romulus.html

Operation Barbarossa: why Hitler's invasion of the Soviet Union was his greatest mistake. (2021, March 3). HistoryExtra. https://www.historyextra.com/period/second-world-war/operation-barbarossa-hitlers-greatest-mistake/

Pagan to Christian: The Transformation of Rome. (2017, April 17). Brewminate: A Bold Blend of News and Ideas. https://brewminate.com/pagan-to-christian-the-transformation-of-rome/

Pandemics and the persecution of minorities: Evidence from the Black Death. (n.d.). CEPR. https://cepr.org/voxeu/columns/pandemics-and-persecution-minorities-evidence-black-death

PBS – Napoleon: Napoleon at war. (n.d.). Pbs.org. https://www.pbs.org/empires/napoleon/n_war/campaign/page_6.html

Persecution of the Jews – insects, disease, and history. (n.d.). Montana.edu. https://www.montana.edu/historybug/yersiniaessays/pariera-dinkins.html

Pirie, M. (2019, May 30). Voltaire, champion of freedom –. Adam Smith Institute. https://www.adamsmith.org/blog/voltaire-champion-of-freedom

Rattini, K. B. (2019, February 20). Julius Caesar—facts and information. National Geographic. https://www.nationalgeographic.com/culture/article/julius-caesar

Renaissance Period: Timeline, Art & Facts. (2018, April 4). HISTORY.
https://www.history.com/topics/renaissance/renaissance

Ritzmann, I. (1998). The Black Death as a cause of the massacres of Jews: a myth of medical history? Medizin, Gesellschaft, Und Geschichte: Jahrbuch Des Instituts Für Geschichte Der Medizin Der Robert Bosch Stiftung, 17. https://pubmed.ncbi.nlm.nih.gov/11625662/

Roosen, J., & Curtis, D. R. (2019). The 'light touch' of the Black Death in the Southern Netherlands: an urban trick: THE BLACK DEATH IN THE SOUTHERN NETHERLANDS. The Economic History Review, 72(1), 32–56. https://doi.org/10.1111/ehr.12667

Russell, E., University of Cambridge, Parker, M., & University of Bristol. (2020, July 2). How the Black Death made the rich richer. BBC. https://www.bbc.com/worklife/article/20200701-how-the-black-death-make-the-rich-richer

Sakoulas, T. (n.d.). The Agora of Athens. This Page and All Its Contents Are Copyright © 2002-today, Ancient-Greece.org. All Rights Reserved. For Copyright Release Information, See the About Page. https://www.ancient-greece.org/archaeology/agora.html

Singh, A. (2021, February 19). The early life of Adolf Hitler. Wondrium Daily.

Singh, A. (2022, April 25). Black Death and Medieval People: Resilience during a Pandemic. Wondrium Daily

Taylor, A. (2011, October 16). World War II: The Holocaust. Atlantic Monthly (Boston, Mass.: 1993). https://www.theatlantic.com/photo/2011/10/world-war-ii-the-holocaust/100170/

The economic impact of the black death. (n.d.). .eh.net. https://eh.net/encyclopedia/the-economic-impact-of-the-black-death/

The Editors of Encyclopaedia Britannica. (1998, July 20). Sforza Family | Italian Renaissance, Milan & Politics. Encyclopedia Britannica. https://www.britannica.com/topic/family-kinship

The Editors of Encyclopaedia Britannica. (2023, March 10). Council of Five Hundred | Athens, Ancient Greece, & Definition. Encyclopedia Britannica. https://www.britannica.com/topic/Council-of-Five-Hundred-ancient-Greek-council

The Editors of Encyclopedia Britannica. (2011). Roman republican calendar. In Encyclopedia Britannica.

The Editors of Encyclopedia Britannica. (2023). Treaty of Tordesillas. In Encyclopedia Britannica.

The Great Courses. (2017, December 1). Caesar's road to the Rubicon—Rome goes to war. Wondrium Daily.

The Great Courses. (2017, October 12). Who was Napoleon Bonaparte? The Early Years. Wondrium Daily.

The Julian calendar takes effect for the first time on New Year's Day. (2010, July 21). HISTORY. https://www.history.com/this-day-in-history/new-years-day

The Munich Putsch – The Holocaust Explained: Designed for schools. (n.d.). Theholocaustexplained.org. https://www.theholocaustexplained.org/the-nazi-rise-to-power/the-early-years-of-the-nazi-party/the-beer-hall-putsch/

The Peasants' Revolt. (2022, February 25). BBC. https://www.bbc.co.uk/bitesize/topics/z93txbk/articles/zyb77yc

The Rise of napoleon. (n.d.). Studentsofhistory.com. https://www.studentsofhistory.com/the-rise-of-napoleon

The Roman Empire: A brief history. (n.d.). Mpm.edu. https://www.mpm.edu/research-collections/anthropology/anthropology-collections-research/mediterranean-oil-lamps/roman-empire-brief-history

The Roman Empire: In the first century. The Roman Empire. Emperors. Julius Caeser. (n.d.). Pbs.org. https://www.pbs.org/empires/romans/empire/julius_caesar.html

The Romans – Roman government. (2013, November 19). History. https://www.historyonthenet.com/the-romans-roman-government

The Sforza Family. (n.d.). https://www.sgira.org/patrons_sforza.htm

The trans-Atlantic slave trade · African passages, lowcountry adaptations · lowcountry digital history initiative. (n.d.). Cofc.edu. https://ldhi.library.cofc.edu/exhibits/show/africanpassageslowcountryadapt/intro ductionatlanticworld/trans_atlantic_slave_trade

Treaty of Tordesillas. (n.d.). Nationalgeographic.org. https://education.nationalgeographic.org/resource/treaty-tordesillas/

Vernon, J. (2023, March 14). The Ides of March—a day of murder that forever changed history. National Geographic. https://www.nationalgeographic.com/history/article/julius-caesar-ides-of-march

Volle, A. (2023). storming of the Bastille. In Encyclopedia Britannica.

Wareing, J. (2018, November 30). How Rome came to be ruled by emperors. Highbrow. https://gohighbrow.com/how-rome-came-to-be-ruled-by-emperors/

Watts, E. (2020, October 27). Pagan complacency and the birth of the Christian Roman empire. Aeon; Aeon Magazine. https://aeon.co/essays/pagan-complacency-and-the-birth-of-the-christian-roman-empire

What was Operation "Barbarossa"? (n.d.). Imperial War Museums. https://www.iwm.org.uk/history/what-was-operation-barbarossa

When the Vikings ruled in Britain: A brief history of Danelaw. (n.d.). Sky HISTORY TV Channel. https://www.history.co.uk/articles/when-the-vikings-ruled-in-britain-a-brief-history-of-danelaw

Wilde, R. (2019). The Rise and Fall of the Borgia Family. ThoughtCo. https://www.thoughtco.com/the-borgias-infamous-family-of-renaissance-italy-1221656

World war II and the holocaust, 1939–1945 — United States holocaust memorial museum. (n.d.). Ushmm.org. https://www.ushmm.org/learn/holocaust/path-to-nazi-genocide/chapter-4/world-war-ii-and-the-holocaust-1939-1945

Xviii, L. (2009, November 6). Battle of Waterloo. HISTORY. https://www.history.com/topics/european-history/battle-of-waterloo

Zarevich, E. R. (2021, July 1). How the Black Death led to the Peasants' Revolt. Explorethearchive.com; Open Road Media. https://explorethearchive.com/peasants-revolt

www.ingramcontent.com/pod-product-compliance
Lightning Source LLC
Chambersburg PA
CBHW070725130626
46553CB00005B/2152

9 798892 960021